"At last, biblical theology mad[...] gets this much-needed new series [...] y off to a wonderful start with an i[...] n of God through the Scriptures. [...] f the Bible, greater worship of the Son, and greater anticipation of the new creation."

David P. Murray, Professor of Old Testament, Puritan Reformed Theological Seminary; pastor, Grand Rapids Free Reformed Church, Grand Rapids, Michigan; author, *Jesus on Every Page* and *The Happy Christian*

"Goldsworthy has devoted his lifetime's work to helping us understand the organic unity of the Bible. He has had a huge influence on my understanding of how the Old Testament anticipates Christ. I recommend this important work to all readers, particularly pastors and laypeople who want to see Christ in the Old Testament."

Tremper Longman III, Robert H. Gundry Professor of Biblical Studies, Westmont College

"In this focused little book, Goldsworthy does what he does best—he helps us connect the dots that punctuate the Bible from beginning to end. This book provides those of us who may have quickly read past biblical references to Jesus as the Son of God, thinking we have grasped the meaning of the term, with a tour of its variations and implications throughout Scripture, putting it in context of the failure of previous sons—Adam, Israel, and Solomon—so we might grow in the grace and knowledge of our Lord Jesus Christ."

Nancy Guthrie, Bible teacher; author, Seeing Jesus in the Old Testament Bible study series

"Goldsworthy has provided serious Bible students an excellent treatment of why and how God the Son took on flesh to save the children of God for the kingdom of God. Linking New Testament themes to their Old Testament sources, Goldsworthy demonstrates the importance of the unity of the Bible, union with Christ, and hope based in God's coming kingdom. This is a solid beginning to an important series."

Paul R. House, Professor of Divinity, Beeson Divinity School; author, *Old Testament Theology*

"A thought-provoking, careful, and engaging study of an important, and often misunderstood, notion. A great resource for further thinking!"

C. John Collins, Professor of Old Testament, Covenant Theological Seminary; author, *The God of Miracles, Science, and Faith: Friends or Foes?*

"The resurgence of interest in biblical theology owes much, perhaps most, to Graeme Goldsworthy. Who better, then, to inaugurate Crossway's Short Studies in Biblical Theology? And there is no better way for such a series to start than with the Son of God, in whom all the promises are yes and amen."

James M. Hamilton Jr., Associate Professor of Biblical Theology, The Southern Baptist Theological Seminary; author, *God's Glory in Salvation through Judgment*

"Goldsworthy writes with a clarity that is possible only for someone who has reflected deeply on the issues and is a master of his subject. This is not just a fine study of a biblical theme, but an excellent example of sound biblical-theological method. Don't miss the last few pages, which show just how pastorally significant this book is."

Barry G. Webb, Senior Research Fellow Emeritus in Old Testament, Moore Theological College

"There are many rich and vibrant themes that course throughout the Bible, and Goldsworthy has traced the idea of the Son of God with clarity, precision, and discernment. The Scriptures are massive, but with this little book we have a clear line of sight to learn more about the significance of this idea, whether as sons of God or as we contemplate the glory of the one and only Son of God, Jesus Christ. Anyone can profit from reading this study from one of today's insightful biblical theologians."

J. V. Fesko, Academic Dean and Professor of Systematic and Historical Theology, Westminster Seminary California

"In this worshipful book, Goldsworthy focuses on the incarnate Son of God as the climax of redemptive history and considers how his role relates to his also being God the Son as part of the Trinity. This book is for all who treasure Jesus and want to understand better how the whole Bible testifies about him. I delightfully recommend this book."

Jason S. DeRouchie, Associate Professor of Old Testament, Bethlehem College and Seminary

THE SON OF GOD
AND THE NEW CREATION

THE SON OF GOD
AND THE NEW CREATION

GRAEME GOLDSWORTHY

DANE C. ORTLUND AND MILES V. VAN PELT,
SERIES EDITORS

WHEATON, ILLINOIS

The Son of God and the New Creation

Copyright © 2015 by Graeme Goldsworthy

Published by Crossway
               1300 Crescent Street
               Wheaton, Illinois 60187

All rights reserved. No part of this publication may be reproduced, stored in a retrieval system, or transmitted in any form by any means, electronic, mechanical, photocopy, recording, or otherwise, without the prior permission of the publisher, except as provided for by USA copyright law.

Cover design: Crystal Courtney

First printing 2015

Printed in the United States of America

Scripture quotations are from the ESV® Bible (The Holy Bible, English Standard Version®), copyright © 2001 by Crossway, a publishing ministry of Good News Publishers. Used by permission. All rights reserved.

All emphases in Scripture quotations have been added by the author.

Trade paperback ISBN: 978-1-4335-4535-1
ePub ISBN: 978-1-4335-4538-2
PDF ISBN: 978-1-4335-4536-8
Mobipocket ISBN: 978-1-4335-4537-5

Library of Congress Cataloging-in-Publication Data
Goldsworthy, Graeme.
   The Son of God and the new creation / Graeme
Goldsworthy.
      pages cm. — (Short studies in biblical theology)
   Includes bibliographical references and index.
   ISBN 978-1-4335-4535-1 (tp)
   1. Son of God—Biblical teaching. 2. Son of Man—
Biblical teaching. I. Title.
BS680.S66G65   2015
231'.2—dc23   2014044916

Crossway is a publishing ministry of Good News Publishers.

VP		25	24	23	22	21	20	19	18	17	16	15
15	14	13	12	11	10	9	8	7	6	5	4	3	2	1

To my grandchildren:
Jake Goldsworthy
Ethan Goldsworthy
Keira Goldsworthy

CONTENTS

SERIES PREFACE

Most of us tend to approach the Bible early on in our Christian lives as a vast, cavernous, and largely impenetrable book. We read the text piecemeal, finding golden nuggets of inspiration here and there, but remain unable to plug any given text meaningfully into the overarching storyline. Yet one of the great advances in evangelical biblical scholarship over the past few generations has been the recovery of biblical theology—that is, a renewed appreciation for the Bible as a theologically unified, historically rooted, progressively unfolding, and ultimately Christ-centered narrative of God's covenantal work in our world to redeem sinful humanity.

This renaissance of biblical theology is a blessing, yet little of it has been made available to the general Christian population. The purpose of Short Studies in Biblical Theology is to connect the resurgence of biblical theology at the academic level with everyday believers. Each volume is written by a capable scholar or churchman who is consciously writing in a way that requires no prerequisite theological training of the reader. Instead, any thoughtful Christian disciple can track with and benefit from these books.

Each volume in this series takes a whole-Bible theme and traces it through Scripture. In this way readers not only learn about a given theme but also are given a model for how to read the Bible as a coherent whole.

We are launching this series because we love the Bible, we love the church, and we long for the renewal of biblical theology in the academy to enliven the hearts and minds of Christ's disciples all around the world. As editors, we have found few discoveries more thrilling in life than that of seeing the whole Bible as a unified story of God's gracious acts of redemption, and indeed of seeing the whole Bible as ultimately about Jesus, as he himself testified (Luke 24:27; John 5:39).

The ultimate goal of Short Studies in Biblical Theology is to magnify the Savior and to build up his church—magnifying the Savior through showing how the whole Bible points to him and his gracious rescue of helpless sinners; and building up the church by strengthening believers in their grasp of these life-giving truths.

Dane C. Ortlund and Miles V. Van Pelt

INTRODUCTION

Welcome to this study of *The Son of God and the New Creation*. In the pages that follow we will journey through the whole Bible to see how the theme of "Son of God" develops from Genesis to Revelation and also how Jesus as God's Son launches the new creation that we all deeply long for—and, by grace, can be part of here and now.

I consider it a great privilege to contribute the first in Crossway's new series Short Studies in Biblical Theology. The discipline of biblical theology has been a passion of mine since I was introduced to the concept during my initial theological training at Moore College in the mid-1950s. I have preached it, taught it, and written about it for over fifty years. And I find, now as ever, that I continually discover new and exciting insights and ideas relating to the great overall plan of God for salvation revealed in Scripture. The Bible embraces a magnificent unity of God's revelation. But it is also complex and diverse with many important ideas and themes running through the single storyline from creation to new creation.

The unity of the Bible means that all parts or texts relate to all other parts. Biblical theology is the way we investigate these internal relationships within the "big picture." At the heart of this diversity is the great unifying factor of the person of Jesus Christ himself.

As a student, and in my early days of teaching, I was introduced to significant works in biblical theology by Geerhardus Vos, Edmund Clowney, John Bright, Oscar Cullmann, C. H. Dodd, and many others. It did not take long for me to realize the importance of having a grasp of the big picture of biblical revelation. The more I got into this study, the more I perceived how little it was taught or understood in the churches. I found it hard to understand the neglect of this important subject. I became convinced that biblical theology should be taught not only in the seminary but also in the local church, to equip all Christians to read and understand the Bible on the Bible's own terms. I was also convinced that a sound biblical theology should inform the way we teach our children to know and understand the message of salvation in the Bible.

I am confident that Short Studies in Biblical Theology will make a valuable contribution to the formation of Christ-centered biblical interpretation on the part of those who may not have had the benefit of formal theological training. But I have no wish to exclude those who have been to seminary! Biblical theology is really only a formal title for what should be, for all Christians, a normal approach to the Scriptures that is informed by the nature of the Bible itself. Sunday school and discipleship curricula should be developed with the goal of instructing Christians of any age in the way the entire progressive revelation of the Bible testifies to Christ and his kingdom.

This series will, I trust, make an important contribution to the nontechnical literature of biblical theology. There are many books written by academic theologians for other academic theologians. And that is as it should be. But I believe there is a big gap between what is written for academic discussion and what is written for the edification of ordinary Christians. I am confident that this series can address that gap with sound biblical studies on important themes. If the Bible is, as we claim, a grand unity governed by the oversight of the Holy Spirit, then no concept or theme stands alone. Evangelical and Reformed biblical theology proceeds on the conviction that all parts of the Bible have an organic relationship to all other parts. It also asserts that all parts testify ultimately to Christ and the gracious salvation he brings.

I am grateful to Crossway for the opportunity to engage in this study of the theme "the Son of God." I am indebted to the editors, Dr. Dane Ortlund and Dr. Miles Van Pelt, for their careful vetting of the manuscript and many helpful suggestions. I have dissented from some of their suggestions, and, therefore, I must bear the responsibility for any blemishes in the finished product. If I ask readers occasionally to move outside their comfort zones, I hope they will appreciate why I do so. When I consider it necessary, I occasionally go into areas of systematic theology and the history of doctrine. But this is all for the goal of building up my fellow believers in the truths of the gospel.

I know there are many others behind the scenes at Crossway who have worked hard to bring this volume to light, and to them I am most grateful. Also, in my retirement I continue to have the loving support of Miriam, my wife of fifty years, who quietly sees to my needs and has always supported my ministry. To her I am most indebted.

But my greatest debt is to almighty God, who called me in my youth, lovingly made me his own, and gave me this ministry of biblical theology. At least half of my working life has been within the context of local churches. There I have been concerned for the teaching of all ages, especially that of children and younger Christians. I dedicate this volume to my grandchildren, Jake Goldsworthy, Ethan Goldsworthy, and Keira Goldsworthy, with the prayer that they will grow to be ever more confident and competent in their reading and applying the biblical message, and that they will always rejoice in the gospel of our salvation.

1

THEMATIC STUDIES
A Biblical-Theological Approach

The Bible begins in Genesis 1 and 2 with creation and ends in Revelation 21 and 22 with the new creation. That is the simple and direct way of describing the two ends of the biblical story. Between these "bookends," in the story from Genesis 3 through to Revelation 20, we have the account of the fall of mankind, the consequent corruption of the universe, and the gracious work of God to redeem the situation.

Alpha and Omega: Christ and Creation

At the heart of this redemptive history is the towering figure of Jesus and his saving work through his birth, life, death, resurrection, and ascension. It is remarkable that one of the last words from the ascended Jesus himself is this self-description:

> I, Jesus, have sent my angel to testify to you about these things for the churches. I am the root and the descendant of David, the bright morning star. (Rev. 22:16)

The testimony for the churches in these last days concerns Jesus as the Son of David. Why? After all, Scripture also testifies to the fact that Jesus our Savior is God from all eternity, the second person of the Trinity. Why, then, does Jesus focus on his human lineage as one of his last words in the great narrative of salvation?

A little before this, in Revelation 22:13, he has taken to himself the title of "Alpha and Omega," previously applied to God in Revelation 1:8 and 21:6. Clearly, these two perspectives mean that we cannot avoid the fact that Jesus is true man *and* true God. Nor can we avoid the fact that we can never separate these two realities: Jesus goes on being identified as the God-man right through the redemptive story and into its eternal conclusion. In this study we will see this truth as it is revealed in the progress of the story from creation to new creation. At the heart of this story is Jesus, who is called the "Son of God." In this study we shall see specifically how the Son of God is *the author and mediator of a new creation.*

There is a tendency among evangelical Christians to understand new creation in terms of individual regeneration, or new birth, as a purely personal experience relating to our conversion to Christ.[1] If the broader new creation is thought of at all, it is often as something quite separated from our new birth. We think of new birth as a present reality and new creation as a future one. This separation is, I believe, a mistake. We may distinguish the two events, but we should not separate them. This, I trust, will become clearer as we pursue our study of "son of God."

Words and Meanings

"You are the Christ, the Son of the living God" (Matt. 16:16). Peter's confession received commendation from Jesus as hav-

---

[1] 2 Cor. 5:17, e.g.—"If anyone is in Christ, he is a new creation"—is often understood to be referring to the individual becoming a new creation rather than to an individual being swept up into the broader new creation Christ brings. We will return to the text in chapter 4.

ing been revealed to him by "my Father who is in heaven" (v. 17).

Many Christians have formed some ideas about the meaning of the title "Christ." It is a Greek translation of the Hebrew word for "messiah,"[2] yet for many people it is just a label. But the title "son of God" seems to convey the idea that Jesus has a special relationship to God and that he may even be God himself. What should the title "Son of God" mean to you and me as it is applied to Jesus in the New Testament? What did Peter understand by "the Son of the living God," and what was revealed to him by the Father in heaven? Did he mean by it the same as "son of God"?

The title "Son of God" clearly indicates a special relationship between Jesus and God the Father. At first it might seem reasonable to take this title as an indication of the Son's deity, the more so when we reflect on the fact that another title Jesus frequently applied to himself was "Son of Man." On the surface the latter would seem most obviously to mean simply that he was human, since that is the literal meaning of the term.

But things are not always what they seem to be on first sight. This understandable assigning of meanings to the two titles at least has this to commend it: it seems to provide a way of engaging with the historic confession of the Christian church that Jesus is both truly God and truly man. Yet, for many, this understanding of Jesus having two seemingly incompatible natures is a difficulty and even a stumbling block. It seems to fly in the face of simple, rational logic to say that one and the same person can embrace two such complete but different natures in a way that compromises neither of them. The problem doesn't stop there. A school chaplain was once asked by a student, "If Jesus is God, who looked after things up there while he was down here?" Once we

---

[2] The Hebrew word for *messiah* occurs only twice in the Bible, in Daniel 9:25–26 (ESV "anointed one"), although the verbal forms of the root *mšḥ*, to anoint, occur in a number of texts.

start to investigate the two natures of Jesus, the doctrine of the Trinity also comes into view. In fact, we could say that the gospel drives us toward the confession that God is triune. We confess that God is one, yet the Father is not the Son, and the Son is not the Father. Then we compound the problem by including the Holy Spirit, who is neither the Father nor the Son. Yet we are talking about the one indivisible God.

Investigating the title "son of God," then, may seem to be a straightforward task involving the examination of each occurrence of the phrase in turn. But this would leave any possible synonyms untapped. For example, do the Father's words "this is my Son" as applied to Jesus mean the same as calling him "son of God"? Luke suggests that it does, when he links the baptismal words of heavenly approval with the human genealogy of Jesus that goes back to "Adam, the [Son] of God" (Luke 3:21–38).[3]

Furthermore, sonship is expressed by more than one Greek word in the New Testament, including *huios, teknon,* and *pais. Pais* is often translated as "servant," and its application to Jesus does not appear to emphasize sonship but rather his role as obedient servant. The sonship word most frequently used of Jesus is *huios.* John uses *teknon* to refer to believers as sons of God, but this is surely not completely identical to the relationship that Jesus has with the Father (John 1:12; 1 John 3:1–2). Yet it certainly raises the question about the link between the sonship of Jesus and our sonship. We will reflect on the nature of our sonship in chapter 4 of this study.

The aim of this volume is to investigate the title "Son of God" and other related sonship titles in order to deepen our appreciation of the person and work of Jesus of Nazareth. We will see that we cannot study these titles of Jesus without becoming

---

[3] The Greek has "son" only in Luke 3:23; thereafter it is implied in the sequence thus: "of Heli, of Matthat, of Levi," etc.

deeply and personally involved since we, as believers, are defined by our relationship to Jesus. But there are some pitfalls we must avoid. Studies that take up a particular biblical theme can either help us to focus on the sense of the overall unity of the Bible or, unfortunately, serve to isolate the chosen theme from that unity and thus undermine the very thing we want to understand. This mistake can result from an approach to word studies that suffers from the mistaken belief that a particular word or phrase is always used consistently and uniformly throughout Scripture, so that all we need to do is establish a kind of uniform dictionary definition. Focusing on a word or phrase also may easily overlook the same concept expressed by other words or phrases.

There are multiple mistakes, then, to avoid in a study such as this one. First is the notion that the chosen word or phrase always has the same meaning; second, that this meaning is only ever expressed by that one word or phrase. The matter is complicated by the variety of ways that words and phrases have come to be translated in the various English versions of the Bible. Sometimes important words or phrases used in earlier documents are picked up and repeated in later documents to make a significant link. A particular title, for example, may appear to be preserved in the actual words for a purpose.

So, for instance, "son of man" literally translates both the Hebrew and Aramaic expressions that mean "human being." But translating the phrase as "human being" or "mortal" in Daniel 7:13 arguably obscures the reason for Jesus calling himself "the Son of Man" in many places in the Gospels (in which Jesus appears to be picking up the specific language of Daniel 7). The way he uses the term suggests that he is claiming to be the figure referred to by Daniel. And in Daniel, the son of man is not any mere mortal but a uniquely majestic figure. And yet in Ezekiel there are a number of references to "son of man" that designate the prophet himself as a human being (e.g., Ezek. 2:1, 3, 6, 8; 3:1). These are not references to the visionary man in heaven as they are in Daniel.

How, then, do we avoid errors of this kind? First, let it be said that there is nothing wrong with beginning with a prelimi- nary investigation of the way in which a significant phrase, in this case "son of God,"[4] is used throughout Scripture. There is a well-known adage that applies here: A text without its context is a pretext.[5] In other words, it is possible to prove anything from the Bible by taking a verse out of context. Therefore the question that demands an answer is this: What is the context of any biblical text that discourages its use as a pretext? We are challenged in this to consider our views on the unity of the Bible. The wider context of a word or phrase is what helps us determine its meaning. Usage is more revealing than some static dictionary definition.

The Unity of the Bible

Is the Bible, as some would assert, a collection of sixty-six books so loosely related that their unity is not a real consid- eration? Or is it a collection displaying diversity within an inescapable organic unity?

If we take the latter view, we still have to decide on the na- ture of the unity. Why did the Christian church come to receive these various books, and not others, as Scripture? If there is a real organic unity to the contents of the biblical books, it follows that the broadest context of any given text is the whole Bible. This, of course, does not mean that the place of a text within smaller units is unimportant. Immediate literary units (e.g., a parable or a pro-

---

[4] Where the reference is to Jesus, I use the capitalized form "Son," and where not referring to Jesus, I use "son."

[5] An isolated text does not necessarily become a pretext, but it is easily used as one.

phetic oracle), whole pericopes[6] (e.g., the Noah narrative, Luke's birth narrative, the Sermon on the Mount), the book in which our text occurs, and the entire canon of Scripture are aspects of the ever-widening context that shapes the meaning of a text.[7]

This is not the place to give a detailed treatment of how the Bible can be regarded as a unity. Still, it is one of the functions of biblical theology to help us articulate the nature of this unity. The canonical process (that is, the way in which the Bible came to be composed of certain books and not others), which took some time to complete, must surely have involved certain assumptions about why these sixty-six books should be regarded as the Scriptures of the Christian church. And yet the diversity within the canon of Scripture is more obvious: the various books were written in three different languages over a period of more than fifteen hundred years. The biblical books also display a large variety of literary genres or types, all of which have their own characteristics that affect the way we read and understand them. Some three-quarters of the total bulk of the Bible—what we call the "Old Testament"—deal with a religion that predates the coming of Jesus. Therefore only the final quarter of the Bible, the New Testament, is distinctly and transparently Christian.

But the New Testament is full of quotes and allusions that show that the two Testaments are intimately connected. Indeed, it is clear that Jesus, the apostles, and the early church regarded the Old Testament itself as Christian Scripture. In addition to the general historical continuity, *the heart of this unity of the Testaments is the person and work of Jesus of Nazareth*. He is not only the central character and principal concern of the New Testament, but

---

[6] A pericope is a more or less self-contained portion of the text.

[7] Kevin Vanhoozer refers to "a series of expanding interpretive frameworks." K. J. Vanhoozer, "Exegesis and Hermeneutics," in *New Dictionary of Biblical Theology*, ed. T. D. Alexander and B. S. Rosner (Downers Grove, IL: InterVarsity, 2000), 62.

he is also regarded by the New Testament as the fulfillment of, and even the reason for, the Old Testament. In a very important way, Jesus is regarded as what the Old Testament is about (Luke 24:27, 44; John 5:39–46).

Investigating words and their meanings, whether in the Old or the New Testament, is therefore an exercise in understanding their relationship to the person and work of Jesus Christ. In this study we will examine something of the momentum in the Old Testament that leads us to Jesus Christ in the Gospels, as we reflect together on the whole-Bible theme "son of God."

A Strategy for a Thematic Biblical Theology

For the investigation of any biblical theme, I favor what I would describe as a gospel-driven or gospel-centered approach to biblical theology. Since we begin our Christian journey by coming to faith in the person and work of Jesus, it makes sense to begin with him. Who and what is it that we put our trust in for our salvation and our Christian growth to maturity?

If we start here, we are in a better position to link our investigation with our own personal relationship to God through Christ. Furthermore, since the object of our faith is the person and work of Jesus—his living, dying, and rising for us and our salvation—then explicitly connecting our investigation to our own faith in him renders our study all the more personally meaningful.

This does not mean we are motivated primarily by our personal interest in the matter, for we seek the glory of God in all this. Our personal participation should not be corrupted to become a self-serving, subjectivistic, and wholly introspective exercise. And yet we are intimately, personally involved through our own faith in Christ. The way forward, here, is to ask this question above all others: How does this text testify to Jesus? rather than: What does this text say about us? The latter question is valid but is secondary to the former.

The approach I am proposing and intend to follow in this study is as follows:[8]

1) Make preliminary contact with the chosen theme in the New Testament as it relates to Jesus and his ministry. As Christian believers we are thus personally linked with our investigations from the outset.

2) Identify any ways that Jesus, the apostles, and the New Testament authors relate this theme to its beginnings and its developing background in the Old Testament. We thus begin to engage with the person of Jesus on the Bible's own terms, that is, as the fulfiller of the Old Testament.

3) Trace the development of the theme along the lines of redemptive history in the Old Testament. We may find other related themes that illuminate our central theme and that contribute to the richness of its meaning in the context of the progressive revelation. It is important that we understand how God's plans for his people and the world are progressively revealed. I suggest a basic structure to redemptive-historical revelation as follows:[9]

   i) Revelation of the structure of redemption in the historical events of the people of God in the Old Testament. This is the source of "typology," that is, how people, events, and institutions create patterns that ultimately foreshadow and are fulfilled in Christ.

---

[8] See Diagram 1.

[9] See Table 1. I have expanded on this approach and explained something of its origins for me in my book *Christ-Centered Biblical Theology: Hermeneutical Foundations and Principles* (Downers Grove, IL: InterVarsity, 2012).

ii) Revelation of the structure of redemption in the prophetic eschatology[10] as it comments on the past history
of God's people and recapitulates (that is, repeats, but
with heightened intensity) its redemptive structure in the
projected future day of the Lord in which all God's plans
are envisaged as being finally worked out. This provides
confirmation of the typology within redemptive history.

iii) Revelation of the structure of redemption in the person
and work of Jesus Christ. The revelation of God's kingdom and of salvation that had its typological expression in
(i) above, and is confirmed in the prophetic eschatology in
(ii) above, is now declared to be fulfilled in Christ. (This
fulfillment of the type is referred to as the "antitype.")

According to the nature of the theme under investigation, the
study of its use in the New Testament may require a further distinction being made between the three stages or modes of fulfillment in Christ. These are concerned respectively with:

a) what Jesus did *for* us in the past, historical gospel event
in fulfillment of the promises of the Old Testament;

b) what the word of Jesus and his Spirit go on doing *in*
us as we live in the present our life of faith and in the
world as the gospel is proclaimed; and

c) what the end-time consummation *with* us will be when
Jesus returns in glory to judge the living and the dead
and to bring in the fullness of his kingdom.

This way of distinguishing the work of Jesus as "for us," "in us,"
and "with us" is simply another way of distinguishing our justi-

---

[10] Eschatology (Gk. *eschatos*, "last") refers to the end times and, more broadly, the future events
in redemptive history.

fication (in the past), our sanctification (in the present), and our glorification (in the future). It is what we express when we say, "I have been saved, I am being saved, and I will be saved."

The structure of the biblical metanarrative,[11] then, is important for any biblical-theological investigation. The Bible's timeline involves a progression from the remote past event of the creation, through the early history leading to Abraham's call, and then through the history of Israel. We reach the end of the Old Testament period, however, without a resolution to the prophetic expectations of the coming of the kingdom of God.

The New Testament continues the progression with the account of Jesus: his life, death, resurrection, and ascension. The New Testament presents Jesus as the fulfillment of all the expectations of the Old Testament (the Gospels). Then come the apostolic witness and ministry to the first churches (the Epistles) and the final visions of the end (Revelation). There is clearly a dynamic not merely of historical events but of progressive revelation of God's plan and purposes. This dynamic means that we must always consider the words and phrases that are the objects of our examination not in static, abstract terms but within a progressive redemptive revelation[12] that may indicate a developing understanding of these words and phrases. This means that not all parts of the Bible bear the same exact relationship to us in our Christian walk.

As we examine our subject and related themes, we bear in mind the structure of redemptive revelation. While we will start with the gospel as it is presented in the New Testament, we then go back to the Old Testament to try to understand the foundations of our theme

---

[11] *Metanarrative* is a technical term used to refer to the big picture or overall narrative of the Bible. It includes more than a historian would include since it takes in the whole story from creation to the new creation as the Bible presents it. It is thus the framework for all the biblical books, including those that are not specifically narrative in terms of genre.

[12] I am using *redemptive revelation* as synonymous with the term *salvation history*. Texts from different parts of this progressive revelation will bear different relationships to the person of Christ and to us.

as we now find it in the New Testament. Then we return to the New Testament with an enhanced understanding of the depth and many-sided nature of our theme. This enhanced understanding then forms the basis for a renewed study using the same basic process. And so on!

Summary and Conclusion

Words and phrases that may form the basis of a biblical theme are not necessarily used uniformly throughout Scripture. Usage is an elastic thing, and how one writer uses a particular word or phrase can depend on many things.

For example, the meaning of words or phrases that are the subject of such a study as this may be affected by the developing redemptive-historical context of the biblical metanarrative. Consequently, where the words or phrases occur in the biblical story will affect their significance and meaning. We also recognize that other words and phrases may carry the same or closely related concepts as the principal ones under investigation. In addition, there may be related themes that need to be considered as enriching our understanding of the chosen theme.

Our ideas about the nature and unity of Scripture may need adjustment in the light of our ongoing examination of the text. The redemptive-historical structure of the biblical witness demands that we take account of both the historical story from Genesis to Revelation and the revelation of God and his kingdom that is contained in the story. At the heart of both is the person and work of Jesus of Nazareth, whom we seek to understand better by means of this thematic examination. This is primarily so that our own faith response to Jesus will be strengthened through a maturing understanding of his person, his ministry, and the consequent nature of our relationship to him, to the Father, and to eternity. The ultimate purpose of this study, therefore, is worship.

DIAGRAM 1: HOW THIS STUDY IS PLANNED[13]

Ch. 1. Remarks about the method of this study
Ch. 2. Making contact with the theme in the New Testament
Ch. 3. Old Testament antecedents of the theme
Ch. 4. New Testament application to the Christian life

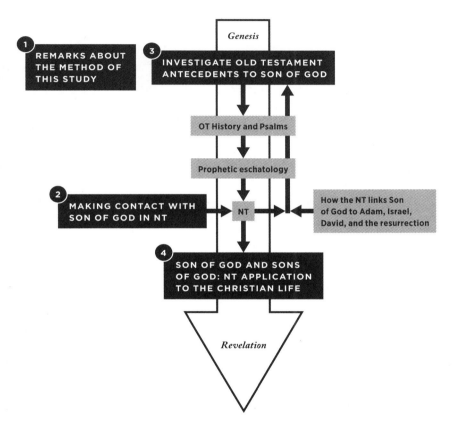

---

[13] I do not wish to imply that the method I have outlined in this chapter is the only way a biblical-theological investigation can be carried out. I have defended this approach in *Christ-Centered Biblical Theology*, but I recognize that there are other ways to undertake such a thematic study.

TABLE 1: THE THREE STAGES OF REVELATION

1. Revelation in biblical history, Old Testament	2. Revelation in prophetic eschatology	3. Revelation in Christ
Creation	New creation	Jesus is new creation
Covenant	New covenant	New covenant in his blood
Captivity	New captivity and exodus	Jesus is the Passover lamb
Exodus redemption	redemption	and new exodus
Entry to the land	Entry into the new land	Jesus: where God and man
King	New Davidic king	dwell
Jerusalem (Zion)	New Jerusalem	Jesus is Son of David
Temple	New temple	Jesus is the new temple, the new Jerusalem

TABLE 2: TEXTS RELATING TO JESUS AS THE SON OF GOD

Son of God	His (God's) Son	"My [God's] Son"	The Son (of the Father)
Matt. 4:3, 6	John 3:16, 17	Matt. 2:15	Matt. 11:27
Matt. 8:29	Rom. 1:3	Matt. 3:17	Matt. 28:19
Matt. 14:33	Rom. 5:10	Matt. 17:5	Luke 10:22
Matt. 16:16	Rom. 8:3, 29, 32	Mark 1:11	John 3:35, 36
Matt. 26:63	1 Cor. 1:9	Mark 9:7	John 5:19, 20, 21, 22,
Matt. 27:40, 43, 54	Gal. 1:16	Luke 3:22	23, 26
Mark 1:1	Gal. 4:4, 6	Luke 9:35	John 8:36
Mark 3:11	Col. 1:13	Acts 13:33	John 14:13
Mark 5:7	1 Thess. 1:10	Heb. 1:5	John 17:1
Mark 15:39	1 John 1:3, 7	Heb. 5:5	1 Cor. 15:28
Luke 1:32, 35	1 John 3:23	2 Pet. 1:17	Heb. 1:2, 8
Luke 4:3, 9, 41	1 John 4:9, 10, 14	Rev. 21:7	Heb. 3:6
Luke 8:28			Heb. 5:8
Luke 22:70			Heb. 7:28
John 1:34, 49			1 John 2:22, 23, 24
John 3:18			1 John 5:9, 10, 11, 12
John 10:36			
John 11:4, 27			
John 19:7			
John 20:31			
Acts 8:37			
Acts 9:20			
Rom. 1:4			
2 Cor. 1:19			
Gal. 2:20			
Eph. 4:13			
Heb. 4:14			
Heb. 6:6			
Heb. 7:3			
Heb. 10:29			
1 John 3:8			
1 John 4:15			
1 John 5:5, 12, 13, 20			
2 John 3, 9			
Rev. 2:18			

2

JESUS THE SON OF GOD
The New Testament Testimony

Our concern in this volume is to understand the meaning and significance of the title given to Jesus as the Son of God. But Jesus as "son" is referred to in a variety of ways.

We cannot simply assume the meaning of these designations, or the relationships between them, without examining how they are used in the various books of the New Testament.

So, for example, Jesus is spoken of as:

Son of God;
"My [God's] beloved Son";
The Son;
His (God's) Son;
His (God's) only Son;
The only Son of God;
The Son of Man;
The Son of David;
The Son of Abraham;
Firstborn son;

> "My son";
> The carpenter's son;
> The Son of the Highest;
> The son of Joseph;
> The Christ, the Son of God.

Clearly, the designation "son" is used in a variety of ways. Along with this list we must also consider the fact that "son" implies a "father." If Jesus refers to God as his Father, or a New Testament author refers to "the Father" as the father of the Son, how is this different from the title "son of God"? That is, does "the Son" (of the Father) mean the same as "son of God"?

Initial Contact in the Gospel Event

Some have treated the divine names of relationship as having been assigned by us humans as analogies of our human relationship titles. Thus, it is claimed that biblical authors have applied the title "Father" to God simply because of the patriarchal structures in human society. But when Paul said, "For this reason I bow my knees before the Father, from whom every family in heaven and on earth is named" (Eph. 3:14–15), he indicated that it works the other way around. God has named himself as Father, and our relationships are named after his. Thus, we are not at liberty to bow to those pressures that intend to change God's names nor to designate him using feminine pronouns (she, her) in the name of evenhandedness. The biblical writers are completely consistent in this regard. Even when feminine metaphors are used of Jesus or God, feminine pronouns are never used.[1]

Not all of the sonship designations that are applied to Jesus have identical meanings. For example, Jesus being called the "Son

---

[1] See, e.g., Deut. 32:18; Pss. 22:9; 123:1–2; Isa. 42:14; 49:15; 66:13; Luke 13:34. God is of course never referred to as "Mother." Cf. Alvin F. Kimel Jr., "The God Who Likes His Name: Holy Trinity, Feminism, and the Language of Faith," *Interpretation* 45 (1991): 147–58.

of God" is very different from the designation "Son of Abraham" or "Son of David." "Son of God" seems also to be somewhat removed from "Son of Man." We note also that the early Christian church, certainly as it wrestled with the nature of God as Trinity, came to speak of the second person of the Godhead as "God the Son" or, simply, "the Son." The question, then, is: does "God the Son," a term not found in the Bible, mean exactly the same thing as "son of God?" If Christ preexisted from all eternity as God the Son, did he also exist from eternity as Son of God? Are these two titles completely synonymous and interchangeable? I do not think so.

Let's begin by noting that some of the above listed "son" titles as they are applied to Jesus do appear to be broadly synonymous. Does this mean that there are no elements of distinction at all in such cases? And between those that appear to be only remotely related, what discernible connection is there beyond the obvious one that they are used of the same person, Jesus? Does not the Word becoming flesh (the incarnation) distinguish between the eternal Son and the incarnate Son (John 1:14)? After all, except in the mind and purpose of God, Jesus of Nazareth was not eternally incarnate but became such at a specific point in history.

Since we are examining the terminology as it is applied to Jesus, the unity of meaning will depend on the answers we give to at least two questions. First, there is the question of individual usage in each literary corpus. Does John's Gospel, for example, reflect a consistent meaning for each sonship title? Second, we must ask if there is a consistent meaning given to the title across the range of New Testament literature. But even if there are nuances of meaning, or even quite marked differences in meaning within some individual documents, what can we then conclude on the basis of our assumptions regarding the unity of the whole Bible as the Spirit-inspired and, thus, self-consistent testimony to Jesus?

In tackling these questions, I want to stress again that this is not a purely academic exercise. Understanding the significance of the titles of Jesus is vitally important practically and spiritually for all Christians. To give an illustration: You are driving on a country road and come to a bridge over a swollen river that you have never crossed before. Do you ask, "Do I have enough faith to drive over the bridge?" Surely not! You would be more inclined to ask something like: "Is this bridge able to support me and my vehicle?" That is, you would be concerned not with the strength of your faith in the bridge but with the strength of the bridge itself as the object of your faith. Consider the application to our Christian lives of the parable of Jesus in Matthew 7:24–27, the house built on the rock. The question is not about me and the strength of my faith but about the word of Jesus the rock and his ability to hold us firmly and safely against the storms of life and death.

My point is that the titles of Jesus tell us much about him and make up part of the New Testament teaching about his power to save. Understanding the significance of his titles is of great importance if we are to confirm our confidence in the saving power of Jesus.

Before we turn to the relevant texts, let me be crystal clear about the assumptions with which I as an evangelical read the Bible. I would not be motivated to undertake this investigation without already having formed for myself some doctrine of Scripture and certain convictions about Jesus and salvation. First, I accept that the whole canon of Scripture as it has been received by the Christian church is the very word of God. Second, although the sixty-six books represent many authors, overall there is the supervision and inspiration of the Holy Spirit of God, so that what the Bible says is what God says. Third, the testimony of Jesus, the apostles, and the New Testament authors is that the unity of the Bible exists primarily at the level of the Spirit's testimony to

Christ. This latter assumption implies a concern to understand the nature of the relationship between the two Testaments and, specifically, in what sense the Old Testament can be regarded as Christian Scripture.

Faith in Jesus Means Engaging the Old Testament

Alan Richardson designates four ways that "son of God" is used in the literature prior to the Gospels in the New Testament.[2] These are references to: (1) angelic sons of God (e.g., Gen. 6:2; Job 38:7); (2) righteous men (mostly in Jewish wisdom literature written between the time of the Testaments[3]); (3) Israel (Ex. 4:22); and (4) the king (2 Sam. 7:14). It is to Israel and its king that the New Testament mainly directs us.

This series of Short Studies in Biblical Theology proceeds on the assumption that every Christian believer needs to "grow in the grace and knowledge of our Lord and Savior Jesus Christ" (2 Pet. 3:18). Every pastor and church leader can probably relate some experiences of Christians in need of pastoral care because of a crisis of faith. My own experience suggests to me that when a Christian goes through such a crisis, it is often because of a superficial, or even erroneous, understanding of who Jesus is and what he has accomplished for us—which we understand only when we take into account the entire biblical witness to Jesus, Old Testament and New. Since the whole Bible points us to the unique person and work of Christ, our first concern should be the power and sufficiency of Jesus to give us confidence in his saving work for us. The sixteenth-century Reformers recognized that the gospel proclaims a salvation that is by grace alone, through faith

---

[2] Alan Richardson, *An Introduction to the Theology of the New Testament* (London: SCM, 1958), 148.

[3] There was a period of approximately four hundred years between the two Testaments. During that time the Jewish faith developed in a number of ways as is seen in the books of the Apocrypha and in the rejection of these books from the canon of Scripture.

alone, in Christ alone, revealed in the Bible alone, and all this to the glory of God alone. The more we learn about the Christ we believe in and trust, the more we will encounter and acknowledge the glory of God.

Understanding salvation or the benefits of the Christian gospel, then, is correlated with our grasp of who and what the Jesus of the Bible is and does. The study of christology, what it means for Jesus to be the Christ, involves the special concern for the biblical data that tell us about Jesus as the Christ. Jesus himself posed the question to the Pharisees: "What do you think about the Christ? Whose son is he?" (Matt. 22:42–46). When they answered, "The son of David," he had a further question that highlights something of the significance of this sonship. The question of David calling his son "Lord" in Psalm 110 is raised. How can the Christ be David's son *and* Lord? This is a question that we must consider. For the moment, let us recognize that there is great significance to what we think about the sonship of the Christ. It affects our understanding of salvation, heaven, and hell.

Because we must reckon with the biblical data that impress upon us the true humanity of Jesus along with the evidence that he is God incarnate, we are forced also to face this question about the "Son of God": is that title the same as "God the Son"? The study of christology must consider what truths we may already acknowledge without ever investigating on what basis these scriptural connections are made.

Thus, when Jesus is shown as fulfilling the Old Testament roles of prophet, priest, and king, he is seen as the mediator, the one who stands between God and an alienated and rebellious humanity. In the Old Testament these offices were all exercised by individual members of the nation of Israel. One of the messages of the New Testament, and especially of the letter to the Hebrews, is that human, sinful mediators foreshadow the true mediator, but they do not themselves mediate saving grace. The true and final mediator, the mediator of the new covenant, made salvation effective through the blood of Christ. This mediator is one who shares the situation of both sides of the dispute: to be both God and man. Paul tells Timothy that "there is one mediator between God and men, the man Christ Jesus" (1 Tim. 2:5). And Hebrews stresses that Jesus mediates a new and better covenant than the old one (Heb. 8:6; 9:15; 12:24).

Jesus is proclaimed as the effective intermediary, or bridge, between God and humanity. For example, Paul begins his great letter to the Romans with a magnificent statement about the nature of the gospel:

> Paul, a servant of Christ Jesus, called to be an apostle, set apart for the gospel of God, which he promised beforehand through his prophets in the holy Scriptures, concerning his Son, who was descended from David according to the flesh and was declared to be the Son of God in power according to the Spirit of holiness by his resurrection from the dead, Jesus Christ our Lord . . . (Rom. 1:1–4)

Here Paul reflects on the gospel in a multifaceted way. He states that the gospel is God's, that it fulfills the prophetic promises of the Old Testament, that it concerns the son of David whom we know is also the Son of God, and that this sonship is declared by his resurrection from the dead.

The evidence from the Bible itself is that the unity of Scripture lies primarily in its testimony to Jesus as the Christ of God. The overall message of the Bible is structured by a history of God's acts of redemption so that there is a dynamic that leads from God's promises of salvation for his people to the fulfillment of these promises in Jesus of Nazareth. "Promise and fulfillment" is a time-honored way of giving some basic shape to the relationship of the two Testaments.[4] This implies a coherent metanarrative, or overall story, which runs through the whole of Scripture so that even the nonnarrative parts can be plugged into this storyline.

A study of any biblical theme logically starts with an examination of the history and promises of the Old Testament for any evidences of the chosen theme. We would then proceed to the New Testament to look at the way Jesus is proclaimed as the fulfiller of this theme. However, I have already proposed above a more personal procedure for our own spiritual growth (that is, starting with the New Testament, then moving to the Old). I do this because of the difficulties many Christians have with the Old Testament. For many, this first three-quarters of the Bible is of little interest other than its being a collection of stories with a "moral" attached to them. On top of this, many other Old Testament stories seem to give entirely the wrong moral message! And then even beyond this, one has to deal with seemingly irrelevant bits of incomprehensible and inappropriate rules and regulations, wordy and repetitious sermons of the prophets, and weird excursions into fantastic apocalyptic visions of another world (such as in the second half of Daniel or in Zechariah).

There are, of course, many Christians who rightly believe that the Old Testament should make sense to them as part of the Christian Bible and that its stories are reliable. But not all of them are sure how it really does work. This situation frequently leads to the Old Testament being largely neglected and relegated to the "too hard and rather boring" basket.

---

[4] Of course, there is promise and fulfillment in both Testaments. But from a "big picture" perspective it remains true that the Old Testament promises that which is fulfilled by Jesus in the New Testament.

I have proposed that we start this study where we all start as Christians—with our relationship to Jesus. Our interest in the Old Testament as *relevant Christian Scripture* is created by our growing knowledge of who and what Jesus is. Put simply: the New Testament declares Jesus to be the fulfillment of the Old Testament. Jesus and the apostles proclaimed Jesus to be the Christ of the Old Testament, and they do this using Old Testament terms.

More specifically, Jesus claimed that the whole of the Old Testament was about him.[5] It has been estimated that the New Testament contains some sixteen hundred direct quotes from, or recognizable allusions to, the Old Testament.[6] If we are interested in the New Testament's testimony to Jesus, we cannot avoid the implications of its preoccupation with the link between Jesus and the Old Testament Scriptures. The idea that the Old Testament deals with the rather irrelevant Jewish background to the Christian gospel is detrimental to the New Testament's exposition of the gospel. Jesus is declared to be the fulfiller, but we won't understand what this means if we don't understand what it is that he is said to fulfill.

Starting with "Son of God"

I have suggested above that it would be easy to conclude that the title "Son of God" indicates the deity of Jesus, while the title "Son of Man" is used to designate his humanity. Understandable, but inaccurate! Let us consider the evidence by starting with the clear uses of the title "Son of God." I will include here an examination of the references to God's declaring Jesus to be his Son and

---

[5] I refer to passages such as Luke 24:25–27, 44–45; John 5:39, 46. I cannot escape the implication that Jesus is claiming that the whole of the Old Testament canon is about the Christ.

[6] So Henry M. Shires, *Finding the Old Testament in the New* (Philadelphia: Westminster, 1974), 15.

of those linking a prophetic word of sonship to Jesus. Although this may seem to go against my stated intention to focus on the specific title "son of God," we soon find that there are indirect references that are in fact linked. Luke, for example, very clearly regards "my beloved Son" spoken at the baptism of Jesus as meaning the same as "Son of God" (see Luke 3:22–38).

Son of God in Matthew

Matthew's first use of "son" is indirect (Matt. 2:15). He quotes Hosea 11:1, words of God that make a historical reference to the exodus:

> When Israel was a child, I loved him,
>   and out of Egypt I called my son.

The reference in Hosea is to Israel as God's son, a term God instructed Moses to use when he first approached Pharaoh:

> Then you shall say to Pharaoh, "Thus says the LORD, Israel is my firstborn son, and I say to you, let my son go that he may serve me." (Ex. 4:22–23)

Matthew applies this historical reference as a prophecy that is fulfilled when Joseph and Mary bring Jesus back from Egypt after the death of Herod:

> This was to fulfill what the Lord had spoken by the prophet, "Out of Egypt I called my son." (Matt. 2:15)

Either Matthew is making an unwarranted use of the Old Testament based on a mere similarity of places and events, or he sees a close, intentional relationship between the two events. The latter is clearly the case. In other words, Matthew is showing us that Jesus is himself true Israel, God's son, foreshadowed by Israel in the exodus from Egypt. Jesus brings to climactic fulfillment the story that began with Israel.

Next, Matthew records the baptism of Jesus, after which the voice from heaven declares:

> This is my beloved Son, with whom I am well pleased. (Matt. 3:17; see also Mark 1:11; Luke 3:22)

Only Matthew records John the Baptist's query when Jesus presents himself for baptism. Jesus's reply indicates that he sees himself as the representative Israel in this event of turning Godward in a baptism of repentance.

> Let it be so now, for thus it is fitting for us to fulfill all righteousness. (Matt. 3:15)

This is immediately followed by forty days of fasting in the wilderness, which almost certainly recalls Israel's forty years of wandering in the wilderness (see Ps. 95:8–11 and its use in Heb. 3:7–4:13). Twice Satan's attacks begin with reference to the claim that Jesus is the Son of God (Matt. 4:3, 6). All this suggests that Matthew recognizes Jesus as fulfilling the role of Israel as son of God. We see this further in the way Matthew, throughout chapters 1–4, frequently takes Old Testament quotations that refer to Israel and applies them to Jesus. Satan's attempts to divert the Son of God from his redemptive course fail dismally.

The situation is less clear in the address of the Gadarene demons whom Jesus casts out (Matt. 8:29). They are soundly defeated by Jesus, but what they understand by their address to him as "Son of God" is not specified. Nor is it totally clear what the disciples understood by the term when Jesus calmed the storm and they responded, "Truly you are the Son of God" (Matt. 14:33). Here is the point to note, however: these and the other miracles of Jesus involve demonstrations of the dominion of the Son of God over creation and thus reflect the dominion given originally to Adam, the original son of God. Matthew presents Jesus as the new Adam who is restoring the rule of mankind over the creation and over the powers of evil.

Peter's confession—"You are the Christ, the Son of the living God"—does not by itself mean that Peter understood that Jesus is God (Matt. 16:15–16). In fact, none of these recorded "son of God" statements do. However, we must take account of Matthew as the theologian who surely understood better than all of us that Jesus is the king of Israel who rules the creation. The background to the title "Christ" lay in the promises of the Old Testament concerning the "anointed one" (which is what "Christ" and "messiah" literally mean) in the purposes of God. None of the anointed prophets, priests, or kings was seen as divine. The expectation of a messiah centered on a conquering son of David rather than on the incarnation of God.

The challenge of the high priest, "Tell us if you are the Christ, the Son of God," would not therefore carry connotations of God come in the flesh (Matt. 26:63). Nor would the crucifixion taunts of the Jews and the robbers be anything more than insulting jeers that strongly contrast with the centurion's expression of wonderment (Matt. 27:40–43, 54). Unless the centurion was a God-fearer,[7] his expression "Truly this was the Son of God" might be considered to reflect his paganism (see also Mark 15:39). But this hardly explains what Matthew wants to convey by recording

---

[7] A "God-fearer" was the term used to denote a non-Jew who had become attracted to Judaism but was not a full convert. Probably referred to in Acts 13:16.

this testimony. Whatever "Son of God" meant, this Gentile got it right and the Jews got it wrong!

Overall, then, the evidence from Matthew does not primarily refer to the idea that "son of God" speaks of the deity of Jesus. It is far more likely that Matthew reflects the Old Testament antecedents in which the title expresses a special relationship between God and his chosen people Israel—a relationship that came to focus on David and his promised son. But Jesus's pedigree goes back even further than David to Adam, the man who, as head of his race, was given dominion over the creation (Gen. 1:28).

Son of God in Mark, Luke, and Acts

Mark's account opens: "The beginning of the gospel of Jesus Christ, the Son of God" (Mark 1:1). However, he leaves unsaid what he means by the title. It is reasonable to expect that Mark will give us some clues to this as his work unfolds. For example, this introduction is followed by two quotes from the prophets that Mark identifies as fulfilled by John the Baptist and, therefore, also by Jesus, whose coming John announces.

Mark's brief account of the baptism of Jesus, followed by the temptation, contains the intriguing comment, "and he was with the wild animals" (Mark 1:13). I propose that this is simply one part of a narrative depicting Jesus as triumphing over Satan where Adam and Israel of old had failed. The result of this victory is that Jesus is seen in harmony with nature, recalling the state of innocence in Eden. Jesus was not in danger of being torn to pieces but was exercising the dominion over the beasts that was part of the mandate to Adam (Gen. 1:28). This also suggests that Isaiah's view of a return to Eden with the advent of the Davidic prince is echoed here by Mark (Isa. 11:6–9; 35:1–4).

The link between Adam and son of God requires further exploration. The point to make here is that the miracles of Jesus are demonstrations of the coming new order that would bring ultimate fulfillment of the dominion role of Adam in creation. Mark, then, shares the overall perspective of Matthew on Jesus as Son of God.

Luke's account puts the angel's words to Mary in a grand redemptive-historical context:

> He will be great and will be called the Son of the Most High. And the Lord God will give to him the throne of his father David, and he will reign over the house of Jacob forever, and of his kingdom there will be no end. (Luke 1:32–33)

"The Most High" is a synonym for God. The next verse declares that David is the child's ancestor. "Son of the Most High" in this case is the same as "son of God." But the angel is specifically asserting the coming of Jesus as the fulfillment of the promises to David in 2 Samuel 7:12–14. Luke 1:32–35 links Jesus with the prophetic word concerning David's son: "I will be to him a father, and he shall be to me a son." We must conclude that *the "son of David" is the "son of God," and that this Davidic prince will fulfill the role of Israel as God's son.*

Luke's account of the baptism of Jesus is unique in that it is immediately followed by the genealogy of Jesus. It is most probable that Luke inserts the family tree here to clarify the preceding identity of Jesus as "my beloved Son" (Luke 3:22). Luke's genealogy is in reverse order to Matthew's (Matt. 1:1–17). Luke begins with Joseph and then traces the line of ancestry back to Adam, the original son of God. Luke, then, wants us to know that Jesus, as the Son of God, is the descendant of Israel, who, in turn, is the descendant of Adam, the first son of God. His baptism, accordingly, is the baptism of the true Israel, the true Adam. As in Matthew's account, the following temptation is of this new Israel, this true and final Adam, and shows that Jesus succeeded in his role of the Son of God where his predecessors had failed. Luke (as do Matthew and Mark) shows the servants of Satan, the demons who torment people, also being defeated by Jesus, whom they recognize as the Son of God. In all this Jesus prevails where Adam and Israel failed.

Another feature in Luke is the juxtaposition of "the Christ," "Son of Man," and "son of God" when Jesus is before the council:

> "If you are the Christ, tell us." But he said to them, "If I tell you, you will not believe, and if I ask you, you will not answer. But from now on the Son of Man shall be seated at the right hand of the power of God." So they all said, "Are you the Son of God, then?" And he said to them, "You say that I am." (Luke 22:67–70)

It seems from this encounter that the Jewish council members understand the terms to be synonymous. It is possible that there are distinct nuances of meaning in each so that the terms are not entirely synonymous, but all are rightly applied to the one person with much the same significance. In this case both Son of God and Son of Man are two related aspects of Jesus as the Christ. The reference Jesus makes to the Son of Man probably alludes to Daniel 7:13–14 where he appears in the council of God, though not identified with God (the Ancient of Days):

> I saw in the night visions,
> and behold, with the clouds of heaven
>   there came one like a son of man,
> and he came to the Ancient of Days
>   and was presented before him.

> And to him was given dominion
>> and glory and a kingdom,
> that all peoples, nations, and languages
>> should serve him;
> his dominion is an everlasting dominion,
>> which shall not pass away,
> and his kingdom one
>> that shall not be destroyed.

Bearing in mind the original mandate to Adam to exercise dominion over the world, the description "one like a son of man" refers to a new, exalted Adam who is given this glorious authority.

Luke, in Acts, records the early apostolic preaching including Peter's sermon at Pentecost. It is interesting to note that Peter refers to Jesus as

> Jesus of Nazareth, *a man* attested to you by God with mighty works and wonders and signs that God did through him in your midst. (Acts 2:22)

The thrust of Peter's sermon is that Jesus is the human servant who fulfilled God's plans for Israel as the true son of David (Acts 2:29–35). Peter's second recorded sermon follows the healing of the lame man. Here Peter refers to the glorifying of God's servant (Acts 3:13), a phrase that may well reflect the same idea as God's Son. He suffers, is put to death, and is then raised (Acts 3:13–26). Although Luke does not provide any direct quote in Acts 3:18, it is probable that he is referring to the suffering servant of Isaiah 53. And the name Christ, which means the "anointed one," points us back to the anointed offices in the Old Testament: prophet, priest, and king. To these is added the suffering servant of Isaiah.

Luke's account of the Ethiopian eunuch's baptism includes, according to some manuscripts, the eunuch's confession, "I believe that Jesus Christ is the Son of God" (Acts 8:37).[8] The only clue to his understanding of this title is Philip's exposition of the gospel, starting with Isaiah 53, which the Ethiopian was reading. The suffering servant is not God but a human who suffers on behalf of the people. We have no knowledge of any prior teaching the eunuch may have received. Paul too refers to Jesus as "the Son of God" in Acts 9:20, but the title is not explained.

Son of God in John

Textual variants of John 1:18 make the reference to "the only Son" problematic,[9] yet he is clearly said to be "at the Father's side." The ESV here follows the manuscript that reads "the only God" with the implication that the Son is God. However, John the Baptist identifies this Word become flesh as Jesus, the one who baptizes with the Spirit, and who is the Lamb of God that takes away the sin of the world. The same Jesus he names as the Son of God (John 1:29–34).

When Nathanael addresses Jesus as "the Son of God" and "the King of Israel," Jesus answers, "You will see heaven opened, and the angels of God ascending and descending on the Son of Man" (John 1:49–51). This apparently recalls Jacob's dream when the promise of the land to Abraham's children is reaffirmed (Gen. 28:10–17). We may propose that the two occurrences of "son of God" are linked to the covenant with Abraham and with Israel after him. Nathanael identifies Jesus as the king of Israel, which is a reference to the son of David.

---

[8] See the ESV footnote to Acts 8:36 regarding the omission of v. 37. Even if this textual variant is to be omitted from inspired Scripture, it is still an extremely early attestation of referring to Jesus as Son of God.

[9] See the footnote in ESV for explanation of textual variants.

The conversation between Jesus and Nicodemus leads us to the most famous "son" passage of all:

> For God so loved the world, that he gave his only Son, that whoever believes in him should not perish but have eternal life. (John 3:16)

This response of Jesus to the Pharisee's perplexity over being born "from above" puts the whole idea in the context of Israel's Scripture. He implies that a teacher like Nicodemus really should be able to understand what he is talking about (John 3:9–15). The reference to "the Son of Man" (v. 14) leads to further clarification regarding "his only Son" in verses 16–18. It does appear that Son of God and Son of Man are closely related here, if not synonymous.

However, John's theologizing on the Son as the one the Father has sent from above emphasizes another dimension. He has come from above in a way that corresponds to the heavenly son of man in Daniel 7 (John 3:31–36). Of course, in Daniel the son of man comes *to* the Ancient of Days to receive the kingdom. Jesus's use of "Son of Man" accords more with his ascension on the clouds of heaven (Matt. 26:64). That the angels say of him that he will come again in this manner indicates that his dominion that he receives on his ascension will be revealed in all the earth (cf. Acts 1:11; 1 Thess. 4:16–17). The relationship of the Son to the Father is also prominent in John's account of the words of Jesus following the healing of the man at the pool of Bethesda (John 5:17–29). The Jews' persecution of Jesus was based on the accusation that he "was even calling God his own Father, making himself equal with God" (John 5:18). The truth of this claim was supported by the statement of Jesus that he does what the Father does and that those who do not honor the

Son do not honor the Father (John 5:19–23). Jesus's use of the title "Son of God" in John 5:25 is the one place in this discourse where he departs from referring to himself as the Son.[10] The latter title is couched in terms of his heavenly origin and is identical with the Son of God.

John's use of "son of God" includes Jesus's rejection of Jewish opposition (John 10:36), his explanation of the reason for Lazarus's illness (John 11:4), and Martha's confession after the death of Lazarus (John 11:27). John's stated purpose for writing his Gospel is "that you may believe that Jesus is the Christ, the Son of God, and that by believing you may have life in his name" (John 20:31). Here we come to a key point in John's use of "son of God" language. *While John certainly identifies Jesus with the covenant promises to Israel, his emphasis is also in the direction of the Son being the one who came from above to do the work for which the Father sent him.*

This contrasts with the predominant view of the Synoptic Gospels (Matthew, Mark, and Luke) that "Son of God" is a term with historical links to the people of God in the Old Testament and specifically to Adam and to Israel with its focus on David. Unlike the Synoptics, John refers to David only in the speculations of the Jews about the origins of the Christ (John 7:42). As Jesus disputes with the Jews, his references to Moses and Abraham (John 5:45–47; 8:48–59) are not to claim linear descent from the patriarchs but to express his priority over them.

John, more clearly than the other Gospel writers, looks both ways: back into Israel's history and upward to the one sent from above. In this sense he is the more advanced systematic theologian in making it inescapable that Jesus is both God and man.

---

[10] Jesus speaks in the third person in this passage (John 5:18–29), but the implication is clearly that he speaks of himself.

Son of God in Paul

I have referred above to Paul's Damascus sermons as arguing that Jesus was the "Son of God" and "the Christ" (Acts 9:20–22).[11] Unfortunately, we have no record of the actual content of those sermons. Paul's first recorded sermon was delivered in the synagogue of Pisidian Antioch (Acts 13:16–41). He begins by recounting a brief redemptive history of Israel—from the patriarchs and the exodus down to David. From David he moves immediately to Jesus, who is described as David's offspring (Acts 13:23). The execution of Jesus fulfills the words of the prophets (v. 29), but he is raised from the dead (v. 30). This resurrection fulfills the promises made to the fathers (vv. 32–33):

> And we bring you the good news that what God promised to the fathers, this he has fulfilled to us their children by raising Jesus, as also it is written in the second Psalm,
>
>> "You are my Son,
>>   today I have begotten you."

Also, Isaiah 55:3 is brought to bear in verse 34:

> I will give you the holy and sure blessings of David.

This linking of the resurrection of Jesus to the covenant with David and the promises made to Israel do not support the popular view that the resurrection of Jesus proves his deity.[12] The evidence is the other way: it shows that Jesus, the Son of God, had a human

---

[11] See p. 47.

[12] It could be argued that Thomas's confession "My Lord and my God!" (John 20:28) was a direct result of the resurrection, or it may be that the resurrection confirmed an already existing conviction formed on other grounds. The resurrection does not prove Jesus's deity. Resurrection will be a universal reality and human experience when Christ returns, but it won't prove anybody's deity.

lineage as the son of David. Paul says as much in his introduction to Romans:

> [The gospel of God] concerning his Son, who was descended from David according to the flesh and was declared to be the Son of God in power according to the Spirit of holiness by his resurrection from the dead, Jesus Christ our Lord. (Rom. 1:3–4)

We must conclude here that Paul asserts that the gospel of our salvation concerns the events that specifically involve the Son of God as the human descendant of David. That it is God's gospel and that the resurrection is empowered by the Holy Spirit does, however, involve us in the Trinitarian structure of the gospel event. We are reminded that God is one. But the structure of the gospel is that the saving work of God is achieved through the incarnate Son. We will return to this passage later to consider the role of his resurrection.

Paul's references to "his Son" are to the incarnate Son who dies and is raised (see Rom. 5:10; 8:3, 29, 32; Gal. 1:16; 4:4–6; Col. 1:13; 1 Thess. 1:10). It is the God-man being spoken of, and we are justified in understanding "Son" here to mean the Son of God in referring to Jesus as God come in the flesh. The same can be said of 1 Corinthians 1:9:

> God is faithful, by whom you were called into the fellowship of his Son, Jesus Christ our Lord.

Paul's reference to the Son of God in whom all the promises of God find their "Yes" demands separate comment (2 Cor. 1:19–20). We cannot suppose that the apostles thought of Jesus only as the human descendant of David. The prophets spoke volumes about the coming deeds of God, which we must presume were also fulfilled in Jesus. Just when the apostles began to grasp that Jesus was both God and man is difficult to say. Thomas seems to have gotten the message on the day of Jesus's resurrection (John 20:28). As we shall see in the next chapter, the idea that the work God does is also done by God's chosen or his anointed begins to be formed in the Old Testament. The raw material for a doctrine of the incarnate God is discernible there, but we must leave the formulation of the doctrine of the God-man until after the actual event of the incarnation.

Another relevant "son of God" saying by Paul is found in Ephesians 4:12–13, which describes the goal of Christian ministry as

> building up the body of Christ, until we all attain to the unity of the faith and of the knowledge of the Son of God, to mature manhood, to the measure of the stature of the fullness of Christ.

This may seem to focus on Christ's humanity as the goal of our own, but Paul has already prayed for his readers that they may be filled with all the "fullness of God" (Eph. 3:19). And yet the fullness of God and mature manhood are closely linked since both are the outcome of unity in the knowledge of the Son of God. In Ephesians 1:23 Paul has described the church as Christ's body, "the fullness of him who fills all in all." We must conclude that "fullness" does not mean partaking fully in the divine essence of Christ or God. It is better that we see it as speaking of the fullness that Christ or God gives.

Son of God in Hebrews

The letter to the Hebrews is of particular interest because it contains the New Testament's most carefully sustained expositions of Jesus in relationship to the Old Testament. If commentators are right about Hebrews being addressed to Jewish Christians, this focus is understandable. Moreover, if these Jewish Christians were being put under pressure to turn away from their Christian faith, it is all the more understandable that the Jewishness of Jesus is emphasized. By embracing Jesus, Jewish Christians have not forsaken their Jewishness but rather have entered into its fullness.

We are concerned in this chapter to get a feeling for the way the New Testament refers us back to the Old Testament foundations of the terminology applied to Jesus as the one who fulfills the ancient promises. Hebrews does this by beginning with reference to God's former method of speaking by the Old Testament prophets and his latter method of speaking by his Son:

> Long ago, at many times and in many ways, God spoke to our fathers by the prophets, but in these last days he has spoken to us by his Son, whom he appointed the heir of all things, through whom also he created the world. He is the radiance of the glory of God and the exact imprint of his nature, and he upholds the universe by the word of his power. After making purification for sins, he sat down at the right hand of the Majesty on high, having become as much superior to angels as the name he has inherited is more excellent than theirs. (Heb. 1:1–4)

Jesus, as God's Son, fulfills the offices of prophet (speaking God's word), priest (making purification for sins), and king (creating, and ruling at the right hand of the Majesty on high). But the Son is not only the mediator of God's act of creation; he is also the upholder of the universe. His description as the "radiance" and "imprint" of God's nature seems to go way beyond Adam's being made in God's image and after his likeness. His superiority to the angels is established by reference to his being the Son of God referred to in Psalm 2:7 and 2 Samuel 7:14. These are references to the king of Israel. The author goes on to quote Psalm 45:6–7 and Psalm 102:25–27 as applied to the Son. In these last two places the address is to God. The Son thus referred to is the incarnate God, the Word of God who is the agent of creation and its sustainer.

According to Hebrews, Jesus is superior to Moses not simply because he is a better mediator of God's word but because he is the very Word of God itself. While Moses was faithful as a servant, Jesus is faithful as a son (Heb. 3:5–6). He is also superior in his priesthood to those priests of the old covenant (Heb. 4:14–5:10; 7:23–8:7; 9:11–28; 10:11–25). This is because he is sinless and because his sacrifice of himself actually does put away sin. Clearly, the Son of God who is God incarnate is in view. Only the God-man can achieve what is attributed to the Son of God in Hebrews.

> Since then we have a great high priest who has passed through the heavens, Jesus, the Son of God, let us hold fast our confession. For we do not have a high priest who is unable to sympathize with our weaknesses, but one who in every respect has been tempted as we are, yet without sin. (Heb. 4:14–15)

Hebrews thus illustrates the important fact that though we can distinguish the divine and the human in Jesus, the God-man is such that we cannot separate the two natures. The underlying nature of the person of Christ is a union of God and man without fusion, and distinction without separation. Thus we can speak of the preincarnate "God the Son" as deity. But as soon as we speak of the incarnate "son of God," we are dealing with the one who has a preexistent "history" as eternal God and is also the one whose genealogy is given in Matthew 1 and Luke 3—a history with a definite beginning even if it has no end.

Summary and Conclusion

Matthew, Mark, and Luke demonstrate that Jesus fulfilled the calling and requirements of the people of God presented in the Old Testament—from Adam to Israel to David. "Son of God" is the title that belongs to God's people of whom the final and true Son is Jesus.

In John, and perhaps in Hebrews, the emphasis is also on the man from heaven. The Son of God is the Son of the Father and comes from the Father to do his work. The way we regard the Son is the way we regard the Father; we cannot separate the two persons even though they are clearly to be distinguished. Hebrews leaves us in no doubt that the person and work of Christ, though superior to the persons and works of the Old Testament, are nevertheless defined by them.

The various takes on "son of God" in the New Testament raise the question of whether the term indicates that Jesus is the man who stands as true Adam, ideal son of David, and true and faithful Israel—or does it indicate that he is God? The question is simply put: Is Jesus God or is he man? The answer we are driven to is: Yes! He is both.

These preliminary investigations present us with perhaps one of the most basic perspectives of biblical revelation that emerges from the gospel. If we begin with the four Gospels and follow them up with the apostolic writings in the Epistles, there are two seemingly incompatible truths we are given about Jesus.

On the one hand, he was a human being "born of woman" (Gal. 4:4), and we have no grounds for regarding his humanity as less than complete. Indeed, it can be cogently argued that the biblical record presents Jesus as the only perfect human being since Adam and Eve sinned. On the other hand, there is the evidence that he is also true God, come from above. If we treat these two natures as revealed to us by God, we can deal with them only by accepting both to be true without any contradiction. It is not a case of either/or: is Jesus man *or* is he God? Rather it is a matter of both/and. If this is the case, does this both/and perspective in Scripture emerge with the actual incarnation as a historical event in the womb of Mary, or is it already evident in the Old Testament? We know that the reality of the God-man began with Jesus being conceived by the Holy Spirit in the womb of Mary. But does the idea, present from all eternity in the mind of God, begin to emerge in the progress of revelation in the Old Testament?

The either/or perspective dogged the Christian church for centuries, and it resulted in a variety of major false teachings, or heresies, which tried to solve the mystery of the two natures in one person. The Docetists were Greek thinkers who declared that Jesus was divine but only appeared to have a physical body. As such, he was said to be pure spirit and not fully human. The heretical Ebionites argued that Jesus was merely human and not at all divine; he was the best possible human, to be sure, but only human. The fourth-century theologian Apollinarius thought he had solved the dilemma by explaining that Jesus was not quite human because his human spirit was replaced by divine spirit. The Nestorians accommodated the two natures by posing dual persons.

It took the Council of Chalcedon in the year AD 451 to come up with an acceptable rule for guarding against the either/or fallacy. This formula did not try to solve the mystery; rather, it proposed a way that preserved the mystery of the incarnation by speaking of two natures in the one person of Christ. It asserted that Jesus was true God and true man: of the two natures in the one person there is unity without fusion, distinction without separation. This unity-distinction formula thus affirmed the logic of both/and over either/or in many apparent contradictions. In this way Chalcedon showed that the formulation of the doctrine of the Trinity as one God in three persons was reflected in the gospel revelation of Jesus as one person in two natures.

The created order is not monistic but reflects God's uniplurality in that *unity/distinction* is the structure of all relationships. The Christian who applies this principle finds that it fits everywhere. For biblical theology it is especially relevant in matters such as the relationship of the two Testaments. We have already uncovered many links between Jesus as Son of God and some important ideas in the Old Testament. In short, the gospel of Jesus Christ is largely incomprehensible without some attention to its preparation in the Old Testament. To this we must now turn.

3

ADAM THE SON OF GOD
The Old Testament Testimony

The Old Testament begins with the account of creation, which climaxes with the placing of human beings at the heart of the universe. It is far more important than the telling of how we got here and how long it took, for it introduces us to the very heart of the biblical message.

Adam's Race and the Creation Paradigm[1]

What I mean by the "creation paradigm" is simply this: the Bible presents a picture of creation that was designed by God to contain the pattern of the structure of his future kingdom. The narratives of creation are much more than merely descriptive. They foreshadow the ultimate purposes of God.

This occurs throughout the whole of progressive revelation and reaches its final goal in the new creation, which is the consummation of all things. Essentially, we see from the outset of

---

[1] I use the word *paradigm* rather than a more general word such as *pattern* because *paradigm* conveys better the idea of deliberate purpose in establishing such a pattern.

the biblical narrative the creation of a situation in which God rules over his people in fellowship with them in the place he has prepared for them. It is, as I have elsewhere described it, *God's people in God's place under God's rule.*[2] Every expression of the goal of God's redemptive action to save his people can be reduced to this basic creation paradigm: God, his people, and the place where the two parties meet and fellowship.

The pinnacle of creation is Adam. He is referred to both positively and negatively in the New Testament. Luke's genealogical reference to Adam speaks of him as the divinely created progenitor of the line leading to Jesus (Luke 3:38). Luke is explaining what it means that Jesus has been declared to be God's well-pleasing Son (Luke 3:22). I have already noted that one of the implications of the larger biblical narrative may be the negative one that God's word of approval at the baptism of Jesus indicates that, up to this point, God's other sons (such as Adam and Israel) had all failed to be well pleasing to him.

Similarly, Paul's references to Adam are to his failures, and they function to show that, by contrast, Jesus brings life where Adam had brought death (Rom. 5:12–21; 1 Cor. 15:20–22, 42–49). Adam, as the type, foreshadows Christ, the antitype.[3] Adam and Christ are connected in that both are the federal heads[4] of their respective races of fallen and redeemed humanities. This headship typology also exists in the reversal from the fallen race to the redeemed people of God. Christ the Son of God fulfills as the antitype what Adam, the type, repudiated. Therein lies the story. Luke tells us that Adam was the first son of God, but when

---

[2] Graeme Goldsworthy, *Gospel and Kingdom*, in *The Goldsworthy Trilogy* (Milton Keynes, UK: Paternoster, 2000), 53ff.

[3] The word *type* refers to a person, event, or institution that foreshadows a greater future reality. The *antitype* is the solid substance that is foreshadowed by the type.

[4] By "federal head" I mean representative leadership or headship, by which the one stands for the many (without blurring the distinction between the representative and the ones represented).

we revisit the narrative we discover how it develops from the fall into sin and through the constant failures of the people of God until the true Son of God appears to bring redemption.

The creation account in Genesis 1 highlights the dignity of Adam's race. Humanity is created, male and female, as the pinnacle of all God's creation (Gen. 1:26–31). Although both animals and man are spoken of as living creatures (cf. Gen. 2:7, 19),[5] this first account describes humans as unique in that they were created in the image and likeness of God. Greg Beale argues convincingly that *image* and *likeness* are terms of sonship.[6] Being made in God's image as his son is strongly connected in the biblical narrative with exercising dominion. That God is ruling Lord over all in creation is simply a consequence of his being the creator. By his word he brings all things into existence from nothing and decrees what shall be in the order of things. By giving mankind dominion over the rest of creation God reveals his own prior sovereignty and designates the human race as his vicegerent.[7] Only the supreme sovereign is able to designate or deputize man as ruler over creation. Psalm 8 describes man's dignity as being created a little lower than the heavenly creatures and being crowned with glory and honor (Ps. 8:5).

In the creation narratives Adam is not directly described as son of God, but we can understand why Luke would call Adam this in the course of Luke's genealogy of Jesus. As we have indicated above, being made in the image and likeness of God is the unique description of sonship and dominion. We see throughout the Scripture the focus on the human race as central to the purposes of God. Even after Adam and Eve fail to exercise this

---

[5] In both cases the Hebrew *nephesh ḥayyah* is used, literally, "living souls."

[6] G. K. Beale, *A New Testament Biblical Theology* (Grand Rapids, MI: Baker, 2011), 401. Beale refers to Gen. 5:3, "When Adam had lived 130 years, he fathered a son in his own likeness, after his image, and named him Seth."

[7] One who exercises delegated power on behalf of another; a deputy.

God-given role, it becomes clear that God never plans to consign humanity to the scrap heap. The promise of a future hope and redemption is given in Genesis 3:15 as God tells the Serpent,

> I will put enmity between you and the woman,
> > and between your offspring and her offspring;
> he shall bruise your head,
> > and you shall bruise his heel.

Furthermore, fallen humanity continues to bear a vital connection with God since we have been created in his image, and this image is marred but not wholly lost in the fall (Gen. 9:6). To kill another human being is to assault the image of God. Humans continue to struggle to exercise dominion, and it is corrupted and only partially effective (Gen. 3:17–19). How far the image of God is affected by the judgment that follows Adam's sinful rebellion is revealed in the generations following Adam and also in terms of what God needs to do to remedy the fallen condition of humanity. The history of redemption reveals to us the true nature of the fall. The gospel not only reveals the way of salvation as the remedy for human rebellion but also shows how far we have fallen in Adam and to what heights we are raised in Christ. By providing the solution, the gospel shows us the true nature of the problem. We can now recognize *the vital link between Adam and Christ*, made explicit in the title "son of God." This link indicates the dignity of Adam's race in being created in the image and likeness of God and in being restored to sonship in Christ.

Not only is Adam chronologically the first of those named as the son of God in Luke's genealogy; the dignity of his place in creation is indicated by his dominion over it. When Adam fell, the whole creation fell with him. This link between the status of humanity and that of the creation before God is made clear in

Paul's assertion that the redemption of the fallen creation is dependent upon the revealing of the sons of God (Rom. 8:19–23). May we not, then, suggest that Paul here understands Adam as the first son of God?

Son(s) of God in Old Testament History

The structure of redemptive revelation in the Old Testament involves two main stages.

First, there is revelation contained in the historical acts of God as they are interpreted by God. This revelation reaches a high point with Solomon but then continues in the history of Israel's decline. After Solomon, historical revelation mainly concerns judgment.

Second, there is the revelation in the future redemptive events foretold in the eschatology of the writing prophets. These messages of restoration are given at the same time as the prophetic accusations and threats of God's wrath on an unfaithful nation.

Within the Old Testament history, there are only a few explicit references to a son (or sons) of God. The earliest reference is in Genesis 6:1–8. The sons of God are attracted to the daughters of man and so marry them. Children are born to them. Whatever is happening here, it is portrayed as an expression of evil that moves God to propose blotting out all living things. Who the sons of God are is not specified, and why their marriage to the women is an evil is not explained. The thrust of the passage is undoubtedly the increase in evil that provokes God to an extreme judgment. Perhaps these sons of God are human beings whose actions display contempt for the dignity of humanity. Their actions would thus demonstrate the rebelliousness of the sons of Adam. The only light at the end of this tunnel is Noah, who "found favor in the eyes of the Lord" (Gen. 6:8).

A couple of similar references to sons of God are found in Job 1:6; 2:1; and 38:7. These are heavenly beings, one of whom is the adversary (Satan) who is allowed to afflict Job. In the last of these passages the sons of God rejoice over God's created order. In like manner, Psalm 89:6 refers to heavenly beings (literally "sons of God"). Whatever the significance of angelic beings referred to as sons of God, the title as applied to Jesus is too heavily anchored to the line of Adam-and-then-Israel for these references to greatly influence our understanding of his sonship.

Even though they are not explicitly called "sons" or "children" of God in the opening chapters of the Bible, Adam and Eve are clearly presented as the inauguration of human sonship to God. As we have seen, the creation of Adam and Eve in the image and likeness of God indicates not only the dignity of mankind but also the role of exercising dominion over creation that reflects a special relationship to God. It is worth noting at this juncture that this is a position of sonship, which is a reference to status rather than to gender since both genders are included.

> So God created man in his own image,
> in the image of God he created him;
> male and female he created them. (Gen. 1:27)

This non-gender-specific status of sonship is underscored in later references in Scripture to sons of God. Because there is a clear lineage of the human race, beginning with Adam, and marked by a special covenantal relationship to God, we can at least propose that one way of describing this relationship is sonship. Adam's son Seth marks a new beginning after the slaying of the son Abel. Human wickedness quickly leads to the flood and the destruction of the godless. The son Noah marks another beginning through his son Shem, from whom the godly line eventually leads to Abraham.

Although our concern here is not a biblical theology of covenant, we cannot ignore the role of covenant as a formal way of establishing and guaranteeing the status of an elect race as sons of God. The so-called proto-evangel[8] in Genesis 3:15 promises redress for the Serpent's usurping of the role of God and the consequent marring of humanity's sonship. This may be understood as implying a covenantal relationship. Christians have always understood this passage as foreshadowing the remedy being achieved by the son of a woman. It soon becomes clear that whenever this son is to emerge, the history of a chosen line of humans will dominate the redemptive process. Covenant and sonship will become a permanent feature of redemptive history.[9]

A covenant-based structure continues with Noah and his sons (Genesis 6–11). Then the covenant with Abraham recapitulates the Edenic foundations of redemptive history that structures the whole Bible:

> Now the LORD said to Abram, "Go from your country and your kindred and your father's house to the land that I will show you. And I will make of you a great nation, and I will bless you and make your name great, so that you will be a blessing. I will bless those who bless you, and him who dishonors you I will curse, and in you all the families of the earth shall be blessed." (Gen. 12:1–3)

> Behold, my covenant is with you, and you shall be the father of a multitude of nations. No longer shall your name be called Abram, but your name shall be Abraham, for I have made you

---

[8] Or "protoeuangellion"; so called because it contains the first "gospel" announcement.
[9] A forthcoming volume in Short Studies in Biblical Theology will address the theme of covenant exclusively.

the father of a multitude of nations. I will make you exceedingly fruitful, and I will make you into nations, and kings shall come from you. And I will establish my covenant between me and you and your offspring after you throughout their generations for an everlasting covenant, to be God to you and to your offspring after you. And I will give to you and to your offspring after you the land of your sojournings, all the land of Canaan, for an everlasting possession, and I will be their God. (Gen. 17:4–8)

The promises to Abraham clearly recall the creation paradigm with its mandate of possession and dominion. In the promise of the land we have loud echoes of Eden. Also, sonship continues to be passed down through the generations: God, his son Adam, his son Seth . . . his son Noah, his son Shem . . . his son Abraham . . . and, eventually, his son Israel.

Other factors of the narrative reinforce this reconstruction. Genesis 4–11 is dominated by the genealogies of mankind. Ten times the formula "These are the generations of . . ." occurs in the book of Genesis, five of these in chapters 2–11.[10] The "godly" line of the elect sons contrasts with the fallen line of godless mankind. Genealogies are here established as a biblical way of showing particular theological relationships that are a part of the revelation of God's grace in enacting his plan of redemption. Sonship is emerging as one key way of showing how a significant relationship exists and is transmitted through the ages. The gospel of Genesis 3:15 continues to take shape in these developments.

Thus far the sonship theme may appear to be too inferential to hold up under scrutiny. I have suggested a number of factors in the biblical account that cluster together with the notion of the sonship of God. These include humans made in the image and likeness of God; genealogies; the broader motif of covenant; and

---

[10] Gen. 2:4; 6:9; 10:1; 11:10; 11:27. See also Gen. 5:1.

the dignity, rule, and placement of God's people in God's land. All of these are supported by Luke's genealogy of Jesus, the Son of God.

But with the captivity in Egypt in the opening chapters of Exodus, the covenant people are far removed from the promised blessings in a way that echoes Adam's exile from Eden. Significantly, Israel is now referred to as the "son of God." This sonship emerges as an aspect of God's plan of redemption:

> Then you shall say to Pharaoh, "Thus says the LORD, Israel is my firstborn son, and I say to you, 'Let my son go that he may serve me.' If you refuse to let him go, behold, I will kill your firstborn son." (Ex. 4:22–23)

The plagues visited on Pharaoh and his people put the creation paradigm into reverse by bringing the destruction of all that sustains life in Egypt. The opening chapters of Genesis show creation; the opening chapters of Exodus show de-creation. The miracles of the plagues mock the false deities of Egypt by showing their impotence to preserve their devotees and the land.

So now it has become clear. The relationship between God and Adam with all of his descendants—Seth, Noah, and Abraham—is one that may be referred to in terms of sonship. Many years after the Exodus, the prophet Hosea recalls this event as an expression of God's love:

> When Israel was a child, I loved him,
>   and out of Egypt I called my son. (Hos. 11:1)

Matthew's interpretation of this passage (Matt. 2:15), fulfilled in the return from Egypt of Jesus and his parents, may raise some eyebrows since Hosea refers to a historical event, not a prophetic promise requiring fulfillment. Nevertheless, it does show that Matthew understands Jesus as the Son who becomes the focus of the true and final exodus event.

God's son, then, is collectively the people of God, those who returned from slavery in Egypt. At Sinai, Israel was subject to the word of God that set the parameters for life in the Promised Land. This land is described as "flowing with milk and honey" (Ex. 3:8), a description that echoes Eden. This redemptive event of the exodus is a "new creation" experience for the people of God—complete with the parting of the waters to deliver the people (Ex. 14:21), just as in Genesis 1 God separated earth and sea to make dry land appear (Gen. 1:9). The redeemed are chosen and destined to enjoy the blessings of life in the new Eden.

The necessary new element for sinners is the redemptive event of regeneration or new creation. The captivity and the exodus event are necessary to show that sinners can enter the promises of God only through redemption. In both the creation and the exodus we have the word of God addressing God's son. In both creation events God's word sets out blessings and curses predicated on obedience, and both creations are to lead to an inheritance in the place God has prepared for his covenant people. When Adam and Eve heard the sound of the Lord God walking in the garden in the cool of the day, they hid from him because of their nakedness (Gen. 3:8–11). Now, with a new redemptive beginning the people of God have the promise set before them:

> And I will walk among you and will be your God, and you shall be my people. (Lev. 26:12)

God will once more walk among his people.

Indeed, sonship is only properly experienced when God is with his people and rules them in grace by his word. The covenant relationship is summed up in many places as Israel's being the people of God. References to God speaking of Israel as "my people" are too many to enumerate here, but the significance should not be overlooked. Abraham and his descendants through Isaac and Jacob are God's chosen; they are his son. The particular recurring covenant formula emerges in Exodus 6:7 and again in Leviticus 26:12. It is linked with the redemptive act of the exodus and restoration; God states that his purpose in acting to save is to make them his people: "I will be your God, and you shall be my people." We shall see that it occurs in various forms and mostly in prophetic oracles of future restoration (e.g., Jer. 7:23; 11:4–5; 24:7; 30:22; Ezek. 11:20; 14:11; 36:28; 37:27).

A significant variation of the covenant formula occurs in the important covenant made with David in 2 Samuel 7. In the context of David's expressed desire to build a temple for God, we hear the promise that a son of David will build the temple, and this son will be the son of God. The wording of the prophetic promise leaves little doubt that the national covenant made with Israel is now personalized and focused on the son of David.

> And I will give you rest from all your enemies. Moreover, the LORD declares to you that the LORD will make you a house. When your days are fulfilled and you lie down with your fathers, I will raise up your offspring after you, who shall come from your body, and I will establish his kingdom. He shall build a house for my name, and I will establish the throne of his kingdom forever. I will be to him a father, and he shall be to me a son. (2 Sam. 7:11–14)

We see here that the son of David, who is also the son of God, is linked with the climax to the historical replay of the original creation that God described as "very good" (Gen. 1:31). We know it was the climax for two reasons.

First, though significant and glorious, David's rule was followed by Solomon's enigmatic decline that caused the corresponding decline in the fortunes of Israel and the nation's ultimate destruction. Second, more positively, this Davidic covenant that had its first outworking in the kingship of Solomon is not an isolated thing. Solomon as son of God oversees the greatest expression of the kingdom of God in the national history of Israel. He ruled as God's vicegerent over a new Eden. Never again in the history of the nation do we see a greater expression of God's kingdom in earthly structures than that of the height of Solomon's kingdom (1 Kings 3–9).

This is why we view Solomon as the key high point of the Old Testament, after whom things continually get worse until the coming of Christ. For a relatively brief period Solomon ruled over a land "flowing with milk and honey." It had its focal point in the temple, in the city of David (Jerusalem), and in the land of Israel (concentric circles of dominion and presence). The nation of God's chosen people was represented by their divinely appointed king. The anointed ministries of prophet, priest, and king mediated God's word, God's grace of reconciliation, and God's rule, respectively. The presence of God among his people was represented by the temple.

But it was not to last. During the decline of the nation after Solomon's death, the prophets spoke God's words of indictment against Israel's covenant-breaking and pronounced God's judgment. God's charge against Israel is typified by his word to Hosea concerning his son: "Call his name Not My People, for you are not my people, and I am not your God" (Hos. 1:9). But the oracle of salvation is not far away as Hosea declares God's intention to restore his people *as* his people who will be known as "children of the living God" (Hos. 1:10). And as we saw above, Hosea would later recall the grace of God in redeeming his son from Egypt: "Out of Egypt I called my son" (Hos. 11:1). Hosea's purpose is to go on to emphasize Israel's disobedience and idolatry (Hos. 11:2). Yet the grace and faithfulness of God have the last say:

> I will heal their apostasy;
>> I will love them freely;
>> for my anger has turned from them. . . .
> They shall return and dwell beneath my shadow. (Hos. 14:4, 7)

Hosea thus reminds us that prophetic references to *the restoration of the covenant people refer to the rehabilitation of the son of God.*

The kingdom structure that existed in Eden was governed by the word that created it and was spoken to the first son of God. This word of God set the bounds and character of his kingdom and prescribed the human role within it (Gen. 1:28–30). Subsequent expressions of the covenant reflect the same authority of the Creator and set out the responsibilities of the people of God within the place God is giving to them. The prophetic word about the nation being a kingdom of priests (Ex. 19:5–6) describes a people on their way to the Promised Land. The whole redemptive event of the exodus from Egypt is a fulfillment of the covenant promises to Abraham (Ex. 2:23–25). The formal vehicle for conveying the idea of the kingdom is the covenant. Once again we see the essential kingdom structure is God's people in God's place under God's rule. And the point to emphasize is this: *we can grasp the idea of "son of God" only when we see that it is inseparable from the whole structure of the kingdom of God.* "Son of God" means the people of God *in his kingdom.*

To sum up: the first son of God is Adam, and his sonship continues through the generations of Adam's descendants who are marked out as the elect people and who are under the covenant promises and stipulations. The climax of this historical genealogy of sons is David, who is promised a final heir who will be an everlasting son of God (2 Sam. 7:15–16). We begin to see with greater clarity how it is that Jesus could claim that Moses "wrote of me" (John 5:46).

Some Relevant Psalms

The book of Psalms is one of the Old Testament books most quoted in the New Testament. Two psalms in particular are quoted with reference to Jesus as the Son of God.

First, Psalm 2 speaks of the reign of God's Messiah in the face of organized opposition from the nations of the world.

> Why do the nations rage
> > and the peoples plot in vain?
> The kings of the earth set themselves,
> > and the rulers take counsel together,
> > against the LORD and against his anointed. (Ps. 2:1–2)

This psalm then goes on to express God's derision for these vainly plotted schemes. That they are directed at God's anointed is probably a reference to the nation of Israel and its king. Then the Lord speaks of the anointed one in this way:

> "As for me, I have set my King
> > on Zion, my holy hill."
> I will tell of the decree:
> The LORD said to me, "You are my Son;
> > today I have begotten you." (Ps. 2:6–7)

There is some general agreement among commentators that the account of God's words at the baptism of Jesus is a reference to Psalm 2:7 (e.g., Matt. 3:17). The same applies to the similar words from heaven in Luke's report of the transfiguration of Jesus:

And a voice came out of the cloud, saying, "This is my Son, my Chosen One; listen to him!" (Luke 9:35)

In Acts 4:24–26 the threats of the religious authorities evoke a prayer from the harassed Christians. They apply Psalm 2:1–2 to their situation and ask for boldness to continue to witness. Clearly, they understand the psalm to have its fulfillment in Jesus as the Son of God. In Hebrews 1:5 this passage is quoted along with 2 Samuel 7:14 to show Christ's superiority to the angels. And Hebrews 1:8–9 refers to Psalm 45:6–7, as the Son is addressed as God.

The second example of a messianic psalm passage that is quoted a number of times is Psalm 110:1, which is also the most-quoted passage from the Psalms in the New Testament:

> The LORD says to my Lord:
>   "Sit at my right hand,
> until I make your enemies your footstool."

This passage is relevant to our study because Mark puts it in the context of the Davidic covenant. The son of David is the son of God.

> And as Jesus taught in the temple, he said, "How can the scribes say that the Christ is the son of David? David himself, in the Holy Spirit, declared,
>
> > 'The LORD said to my Lord,
> >   Sit at my right hand,
> >   until I put your enemies under your feet.'
>
> David himself calls him Lord. So how is he his son?" (Mark 12:35–37)

This passage from Psalm 110 is generally seen as the source of references to the ascension of Jesus to sit at the right hand of God (e.g., Mark 16:19). In his Pentecost sermon Peter quotes this passage when referring to the ascension and follows it with the description of Christ's exaltation and honor:

> Let all the house of Israel therefore know for certain that God has made him both Lord and Christ, this Jesus whom you crucified. (Acts 2:36)

In 1 Corinthians 15:25, too, we find an apparent reference to Psalm 110:1 in the context of Paul's teaching on the resurrection from the dead, where Paul speaks of Christ reigning "until he has put all his enemies under his feet." Similar statements are made elsewhere (Eph. 1:20; Col. 3:1; Heb. 1:3, 13; 8:1; 10:12–13; 12:2). Enough has been said about these passages from Psalms for us to see that the New Testament understands them to refer to the son of David, who is also the Son of God.

We have also seen that the Old Testament background to Jesus's being called "Son of God" involves us in a study of the redemptive history of the covenant nation of the Old Testament. Significantly, one of only two psalms with Solomon named in the title, Psalm 72, begins with the words identifying the king as "son":

> Give the king your justice, O God,
>   and your righteousness to the royal son! (Ps. 72:1)

In various ways Psalm 72 points to different aspects of the covenantal blessings of the Adamic race. The royal son is the new Adam and the recipient of the promises to Abraham:

> May he have dominion from sea to sea,
>> and from the River to the ends of the earth! (Ps. 72:8)

> May all kings fall down before him,
>> all nations serve him! (Ps. 72:11)

> May his name endure forever,
>> his fame continue as long as the sun!
> May the people be blessed in him,
>> all nations call him blessed! (Ps. 72:17)

This king inherits the blessings of the Davidic covenant as God's son. But verse 17 suggests he also stands in line with Abraham and brings rule and blessing to the nations as well as to his own people (Gen. 12:3).

Psalm 89 is another that extols the covenant with David:[11]

> You have said, "I have made a covenant with my chosen one;
>> I have sworn to David my servant:
> 'I will establish your offspring forever,
>> And build your throne for all generations.'" (Ps. 89:3–4)

The significance of the covenant with David is that it concerns his descendant who is the son of God and thus can cry to God as his Father:

> He shall cry to me, "You are my Father;
>> my God, and the Rock of my salvation."
> And I will make him the firstborn,
>> the highest of the kings of the earth.
> My steadfast love I will keep for him forever;
>> and my covenant will stand firm for him. (Ps. 89:26–28)

---

[11] The passages quoted above are probably alluded to in John 7:42; 12:34; 1 Pet. 1:17; Rev. 1:5.

This psalm makes no explicit claim to deity in this relationship of sonship, but it remains one of the important pointers to Jesus as Son of David and Son of God. Even though there are no clear New Testament quotes from either Psalm 72 or 89, they both reflect on the dignity and dominion of David's son, all of which is ultimately fulfilled in Jesus.

Son(s) of God in Prophetic Eschatology

The Assyrian overthrow of the northern kingdom of Israel (722 BC) and the Babylonian destruction of Judah (586 BC) together mark the demise of the glories of David's and Solomon's kingdom as the historical Israelite expression of the kingdom of God. The sons of God are the people of God, but neither of these descriptions is complete without the other elements of the kingdom of God: God ruling his people in the place prepared for them. For the son of David to be the son of God, he must stand as the focal representative of Israel, the corporate son of God. Although the original promises in 2 Samuel 7 are not there explicitly designated as covenant, they are clearly of a covenantal nature and come to be understood as such (e.g., Ps. 89:3–4; Jer. 33:19–21).

We need to examine some of the prophetic references to sonship. I suggest that we can go beyond the explicit "son of God" passages to examine some references that involve a special mediating figure of the covenant promises. For example, Isaiah makes some important references to the Davidic covenant:

> For to us a child is born,
>   to us a son is given;
> and the government shall be upon his shoulder,
>   and his name shall be called
> Wonderful Counselor, Mighty God,
>   Everlasting Father, Prince of Peace.

Of the increase of his government and of peace
   there will be no end,
on the throne of David and over his kingdom,
   to establish it and to uphold it
with justice and with righteousness
   from this time forth and forevermore.
The zeal of the LORD of hosts will do this. (Isa. 9:6–7)

Here is a promise concerning the true and final son of David. That he is called "Mighty God" has been taken by some to mean that he is the "son of God," who is understood to be merely a human king. He is thus described as God's legitimate representative on earth.[12] I must agree with Barry Webb, however, who concludes, "The language of verse 6 can apply only to one who is God incarnate."[13] The language of adoption reflected in Psalm 2:7 may well have been how Isaiah's contemporaries would have regarded it. If so, we must follow the progression of redemptive revelation to its declaration of Jesus as the God-man.

Isaiah employs another messianic term that other prophets also use: "the branch":

In that day the branch of the LORD shall be beautiful and glorious, and the fruit of the land shall be the pride and honor of the survivors of Israel. And he who is left in Zion and remains in Jerusalem will be called holy, everyone who has been recorded for life in Jerusalem, when the Lord shall have washed away the filth of the daughters of Zion and cleansed the bloodstains of Jerusalem from its midst by a spirit of judgment and by a spirit of burning. Then the LORD will create over the whole site of Mount Zion and over her assemblies a cloud by

---

[12] So Otto Kaiser, *Isaiah 1–12* (Philadelphia: Westminster, 1972), 129.
[13] Barry Webb, *The Message of Isaiah* (Leicester, UK: Inter-Varsity, 1996), 69.

day, and smoke and the shining of a flaming fire by night; for over all the glory there will be a canopy. There will be a booth for shade by day from the heat, and for a refuge and a shelter from the storm and rain. (Isa. 4:2–6)

Some would limit "the branch of the LORD" simply to that which God causes to grow. J. A. Motyer, however, is justified in understanding this as a reference to the Messiah coming from dual ancestry, since "he belongs in the 'family tree' of both David and the Lord."[14] This cleansing judgment that is integral to redemption clearly recalls the exodus from Egypt, while Jerusalem and Zion point to the second exodus from Babylon.

Another significant passage in Isaiah gives assurance that the blessings relating to David's line will not be lost.

> There shall come forth a shoot from the stump of Jesse,
>   and a branch from his roots shall bear fruit.
> And the Spirit of the LORD shall rest upon him,
>   the Spirit of wisdom and understanding,
>   the Spirit of counsel and might,
>   the Spirit of knowledge and the fear of the LORD. (Isa. 11:1–2)

The stump of Jesse, David's father, would appear to be a reference to the family tree of David that has been cut off by the Babylonian exile. Isaiah assures us that the dynasty promised to David will certainly not be at an end but will sprout again. Thus, the shoot is a reference to a son of David who shall be endowed with all the qualities of an ideal king. When he comes, the land will be transformed into a new Edenic paradise:

[14] J. A. Motyer, *The Prophecy of Isaiah: An Introduction and Commentary* (Downers Grove, IL: InterVarsity, 1993), 65.

The wolf shall dwell with the lamb,
    and the leopard shall lie down with the young goat,
and the calf and the lion and the fattened calf together;
    and a little child shall lead them.
The cow and the bear shall graze;
    their young shall lie down together;
    and the lion shall eat straw like the ox.
The nursing child shall play over the hole of the cobra,
    and the weaned child shall put his hand on the adder's den.
They shall not hurt or destroy
    in all my holy mountain;
for the earth shall be full of the knowledge of the LORD
    as the waters cover the sea. (Isa. 11:6–9)

Echoing the promise of Genesis 12:3, Isaiah declares that the nations will seek him, and a remnant of Israel will be recovered.

In that day the root of Jesse, who shall stand as a signal for the peoples—of him shall the nations inquire, and his resting place shall be glorious. In that day the Lord will extend his hand yet a second time to recover the remnant that remains of his people, from Assyria, from Egypt, from Pathros, from Cush, from Elam, from Shinar, from Hamath, and from the coastlands of the sea. (Isa. 11:10–12)

Both Matthew and Luke use their genealogies to trace the dynasty of David through to Jesus. The miracles recorded in the Gospels are a foretaste of the transformation of the creation that the Son of David brings.

Jeremiah too uses this imagery of the branch of David who will come on the day of salvation:

Then I will gather the remnant of my flock out of all the countries where I have driven them, and I will bring them back to their fold, and they shall be fruitful and multiply. I will set shepherds over them who will care for them, and they shall fear no more, nor be dismayed, neither shall any be missing, declares the LORD. Behold, the days are coming, declares the LORD, when I will raise up for David a righteous Branch, and he shall reign as king and deal wisely, and shall execute justice and righteousness in the land. In his days Judah will be saved, and Israel will dwell securely. And this is the name by which he will be called: "The LORD is our righteousness." (Jer. 23:3–6; see also Jer. 33:14–22; Zech. 3:8–10)

The name of the branch is significant: "The LORD is our righteousness" (23:6; also 33:16). Before this climax, which clearly anticipates the New Testament exposition of justification by faith, several important messianic themes emerge. Preceding these verses there is a condemnation of the false shepherds, the rulers of Judah who have led the people to destruction (23:1–2). Then follows a reference to the remnant, the faithful ones who emerge from the apparent destruction of the nation (23:3). What is predicated of them clearly recalls the situation of Adam in Eden: they shall be fruitful and multiply (Jer. 23:3, cf. Gen. 1:28). The good shepherds will care for God's people so that none is missing (23:4). Then the Davidic "Branch" will reign over them (23:5). Jeremiah places all of this in the context of a new exodus, which he indicates is the return from Babylon, "the north country" (Jer. 23:7–8). That the king will rule wisely recalls the place of wisdom in Solomon's reign before his decline, and as a trait of the Davidic child of Isaiah 9:6–7 and 11:1–3.

What, then, can we make of the son of David, the branch, being called "the LORD is our righteousness"? Jeremiah says that the Lord will one day be identified not as the God of the exodus from Egypt but of the new exodus from the north country and from all the lands of the Jewish dispersion (Jer. 23:7–8). The exodus, as Israel's paradigmatic event of divine deliverance, has clearly become a symbol for redemption and regeneration.[15] Both exodus events constitute expressions of the grace of God: it is always God who acts with great power to achieve the redemption of his helpless people. Jeremiah's words anticipate the fullness of justification by grace that depends on the imputation (accounting) of the righteousness of God as he justifies the ungodly (Rom. 4:5). The son of David, who is also the son of God, is thus a key player in the redemption of the people of God. The exile to Babylon, as with the captivity in Egypt, represents the death of the nation because it involves the removal of the kingship and the destruction of the temple and Jerusalem. It is another ejection from "Eden," another descent into Egyptian captivity. The promises to the Davidic son of God involve the restoration of all these things and are, therefore, a kind of resurrection.

Jeremiah's description of the Davidic covenant expresses his conviction that God is always faithful to his covenant, even in the midst of exile. It is as certain as night following day (Jer. 33:19–22). The covenant promises are as certain as the created order. Jeremiah has been assured that God is faithful in a way that builds on earlier expressions of the grace of God. Genesis 15:6 records that Abraham believed God's promises and that, in believing, he was justified by having righteousness counted to him. Moses told Israel, "Fear not, stand firm, and see the salvation of the LORD, which he will work for you today" (Ex. 14:13).

Every declaration that God is their salvation emphasizes that salvation is by grace alone: God acts to save his people. Now Jeremiah is told that "the LORD is our righteousness." This adds the further refinement in that we are told that redemption is achieved by the very righteousness of God being attributed to his people (cf. 2 Cor. 5:21).

---

[15] The fact that it is now an exodus from Babylon, not Egypt, indicates that the typology is not static. More than one expression of the type may precede the fulfillment in the antitype.

Summary and Conclusion

Luke's genealogy directs us all the way back to the very beginning of the biblical story without which we will not understand the significance of the title "son of God." Whatever the divine overtones in New Testament usage of the title, our attention is drawn first and foremost to the creation paradigm of the kingdom and the sonship of Adam and his descendants who stand under the covenant of grace as the objects of God's saving plan.

We follow the pattern of sonship from Adam in creation to Israel and then to the representative Israelite, Solomon, its king and nominated son of God. The covenant with David establishes the title of "son of God" on his dynasty. This is the high point of the Old Testament.

When we turn to the prophetic projections for the future kingdom of God, the Davidic covenant is prominent. Over and over again the promised blessings are couched in terms of the promises to David, so that a Davidic prince is frequently described as the mediator of the redemption of Israel from captivity and of the future blessedness of the people of God.

This focus on David and his son links the title "Son of God" as applied to Jesus to his descent from David "according to the flesh" (Rom. 1:3). The focus on David, then, also links "son of God" to the notion of a new creation that is closely associated in the prophets with the restoration of the Davidic throne. After the fall recorded in Genesis 3, Eden's renewal is found in the promise to Abraham of a land; in Israel's possession of a land "flowing with milk and honey"; and in the prophetic promises of a new land which is described as a new Eden. The Son of God is the one who brings regeneration and resurrection.

4

SON OF GOD AND SONS OF GOD

We now return to the New Testament to draw on the connections we have made with the foundations in the Old Testament to the title "son of God."

Son of God and the Resurrection (Romans 1:3–4)

We began by making initial contact with the theme of Jesus the Son of God in the New Testament because our faith in him is the reason we are motivated to do this study in the first place. We could not go far without recognizing that the way the theme is presented in the Gospels and other parts of the New Testament faces us with the need to examine its foundations in the Old Testament. The New Testament simply does not allow us to proceed without some effort to understand the associations it makes between Jesus and the redemptive history of Israel. Thus, we engage Scripture on its own terms, and this is one goal of this series of Short Studies in Biblical Theology.

In this chapter we will engage the biblical material that focuses on our involvement with the reality of our being sons of God through faith in the Son of God.

I have already referred to a key passage linking Jesus the Son of God with his resurrection. This is the opening of Paul's letter to the Romans. Let me remind you again of the apostle's words with some aspects highlighted that are central to our theme:

> Paul, a servant of Christ Jesus, called to be an apostle, set apart for *the gospel of God*, which he *promised beforehand* through his prophets in the holy Scriptures, *concerning his Son*, who was *descended from David* according to the flesh and was *declared to be the Son of God in power* according to the Spirit of holiness *by his resurrection* from the dead, Jesus Christ our Lord . . . (Rom. 1:1–4)

Paul describes the gospel that he expounds in Romans as God's gospel, which was promised in the Old Testament and concerned God's Son. Here he does not specify God the Son as the eternal second person of the Trinity but rather the incarnate manifestation of that Son. We can be certain of this because Paul is explicit about the Son's human descent from David.

We have already examined something of the significance of the Son of God as the human descendant from Adam, Israel, and David. In doing this we have had to take notice of the evidence that somewhere along the line in the Old Testament there is a development of the special link between the human messiah figure and God, such that it looks as if there are shadows of the God-man that we now know Jesus to be.

Paul defines Son of God in a significant way, saying that Jesus

> was declared to be the Son of God in power according to the Spirit of holiness by his resurrection from the dead, Jesus Christ our Lord. (Rom. 1:4)

It would be easy to conclude that the resurrection showed Jesus to be God, but that would be to misunderstand what the apostle is saying. Paul has already told us that the Son is the descendent of David according to the flesh. The son of God in the Old Testament was human, and resurrection is, strictly speaking, something that concerns a dead human being made alive again. There are those who want to downplay the bodily resurrection of Jesus and talk about a "spiritual" resurrection that does not include the body. This, in my view, is no resurrection at all. Rather, it is a docetic[1] event that is more in touch with a pagan idea of the immortality of the soul as distinct from the resurrection of the body. The ancient Greeks saw no joy in the idea of a material body surviving death. Rather, they hoped to be free of such an evil encumbrance and to exist in the pure sphere of the spirit. This was probably the reason some of the Athenians mocked Paul when he referred to the resurrection (Acts 17:32).

So how does resurrection declare Jesus to be the Son of God—the descendant of Adam, Israel, and David? We need to ponder this question, because Paul tells us that the gospel he is expounding to us is about this Jesus. Almost every clause in Romans 1:1–4 cries out for investigation, but we have space in this study to refer only to some of the great doctrines that are concerned with what this Son of God has done for us and how his work affects those who believe in him.

In Romans 1:1 we read that the content of Paul's apostleship is God's gospel. It is the gospel that God planned, that God alone can implement, and that achieves what God intends it to achieve. It deals with God's "problem" of how a righteous God can justify rebellious sinners (Rom. 4:5).

---

[1] From the Greek *dokein* meaning "to seem, appear." Docetism declared that Jesus was divine spirit and only seemed to be human.

Verse 2 tells us that it is the gospel of the Old Testament. Some have taken the phrase "promised beforehand through his prophets in the holy Scriptures" to imply that only a selection of special Old Testament passages makes explicit promises that are clearly and directly fulfilled by Jesus. In light of other evidence in the New Testament (e.g., Luke 24:25–27, 44–47; John 5:39–47), this would be a mistake, given that Jesus claims that the Old Testament Scriptures are about him. The foundations of the gospel are located in the Old Testament. Verse 3 identifies the focus of the gospel message to be the son of David. Verse 4 then makes the extraordinary assertion that it is the resurrection that identifies him as Son of God. We must try to understand how it does that.

This passage is not the only one that links the resurrection of Jesus with the Old Testament.

> Now I would remind you, brothers, of the gospel I preached to you, which you received, in which you stand, and by which you are being saved, if you hold fast to the word I preached to you—unless you believed in vain. For I delivered to you as of first importance what I also received: that Christ died for our sins in accordance with the Scriptures, that he was buried, that he was raised on the third day in accordance with the Scriptures . . . (1 Cor. 15:1–4)

Let me remind you that when "the Scriptures" are referred to in the New Testament, that is a reference specifically to the Old Testament. Paul's claim that the resurrection of Jesus was "in accordance with the Scriptures" challenges us again to consider the Old Testament evidence for resurrection.

Here I want to backtrack and pick up the theme of son of God as it brings us to the idea of resurrection in the Old Testament. We discover that the doctrine of the resurrection, and its antecedents in the Old Testament, are all related to the doctrine of creation and the renewal of the original creation in the new creation.

We have already reflected on Adam as being the first son of God (Luke 3:38). In light of the fall into sin in Genesis 3, the doctrine of creation either is doomed to obsolescence or foreshadows a new creation. It is the grace of God's eternal purposes that establishes the latter. The pinnacle of the original creation is mankind with Adam as son of God, created in the image of God, and after his likeness. The pattern of biblical history and the foreshadowing of the new heaven and the new earth are present in the original creation. The account of creation, therefore, is not only about the coming into existence of the physical universe and living things. It actually establishes the structure of the kingdom of God: God's people dwelling with God in the place he has prepared for them, submitting to his lordship and reflecting it in their dominion over creation. Let us remind ourselves that the creation that God called "very good" (Gen. 1:31) was a material creation that included living beings with material bodies.

Such is the context that defines "son of God." The testing of Adam and Eve carries the sanction stated as: "In the day that you eat of it you shall surely die" (Gen. 2:17). Human disobedience precipitated this judgment and, ever after the fall, the human race brings death to the creation. It is a race now doomed to return to the dust from which it came. The only hope is to be restored as part of a new creation. This is what the gracious Creator has ordained from all eternity.

The significance of the creation paradigm is enhanced when we take into account those references to the plan and purpose of God established before the foundation of the world. The whole plan of redemption, the election of the people of God, and our predestination in Christ all exist before creation and form the basis of the history of God's kingdom beginning with Genesis 1. We can take the references to "the foundation of the world" to mean the same as "before the foundation of the world" in the sense of before history began (Matt. 13:35; 25:34; Luke 11:50; Rev. 17:8; see also John 17:24; Eph. 1:4; 1 Pet. 1:20; Rev. 13:8).

God's eternal purposes precede anything we can conceive of as an absolute beginning. Creation is the beginning of the action of God to establish his kingdom. The accounts of this creative act in Genesis 1 and 2 establish a paradigm that shapes human history until the consummation of all things described in Revelation 21 and 22.

After the fall, God's redemptive plan is put into effect among sinful people who are dead in their trespasses and sins (Eph. 2:1, 5). This gracious plan is conveyed in the form of a covenant.

This covenant has various manifestations starting with the implied promise of Genesis 3:15. The covenant with Noah reaffirms the promise that God will be gracious to a rebellious race.[2] The covenant with Abraham promises descendants and a new Eden as their habitation. In this way, the creation paradigm is repeated as it was with Noah. When Israel's children find themselves enslaved in Egypt, the exile of Adam and Eve from Eden is reenacted—in both cases, that is, God's people have been expelled from God's place. But the grace of God is demonstrated in his keeping faith with the covenant made with Abraham. Thus, while the exile of his descendants into Egypt recalls the ejection of Adam and Eve from Eden, Israel's redemptive exodus brings about a "new creation" of the nation and eventual possession of the Promised Land. In the course of this "new creation," Israel is declared to be God's firstborn son (Ex. 4:22–23). Even though Adam is the first son of God, Israel is now God's firstborn son

---

[2] Both the words for "grace" (Heb. *ḥēn*) and "covenant" (Heb. *bʳrit*) occur for the first time in the Noah narrative, in Gen. 6:8 and 9:8 respectively.

in the emergence of the redemptive new creation in the exodus. The land flowing with milk and honey is for the son of God to dwell in and to have dominion over. As in Eden, there are sanctions. Faithful obedience is rewarded by the riches of the land and dominion over enemies (Deut. 28:1–14). But disobedience brings deprivation, death, and destruction (Deut. 28:15–68).

Eventually the king, who represents the nation, is declared to be son of God (2 Sam. 7:14). The covenant promise is now focused on the one who represents the many. It is thus individualized so that "you shall be my people" is now expressed as "he shall be to me a son." This is not one man for himself but one for the many, expressing the important biblical principle that Jesus is the one who lives and dies for the many (sometimes called "corporate solidarity").

But Israel's permanent enjoyment of the kingdom in the land is denied because of its disobedience and idolatry. A brief period during Solomon's reign is seen as truly blessed (1 Kings 4:20–34). Yet even the blessings of Solomon's reign are short-lived because of his unfaithfulness (1 Kings 11:1–12). Solomon's successors show themselves to be the false shepherds of God's flock. Once again the exile from Eden is repeated in the subsequent exiles to Assyria and Babylon. Once again the sentence of death on God's son seems to be the end of all blessings. When the son of God repudiates his role and status, everything falls apart just as it did when the first son of God rebelled in Eden.

The prophetic promises make clear that this death of Israel in the exile is not the end. The grace shown to Adam, Abraham, and Israel in Egypt will one day be shown to the exiles in Babylon. The prophets gather up all the creation themes and speak of another redemptive event that will achieve what the previous exodus did not or could not achieve. The prophetic oracles of salvation bring many and varied images of renewal. These promises involve the creation paradigm in all its elements that will be fulfilled on the great day of the Lord.

We need not repeat the discussion from the previous chapter. However, let us be reminded that the prophets envisage the renewal of all things. Specifically, the new creation includes a new heaven and earth, a new people consisting of the faithful remnant gathered from the lands of exile, and a new Eden. There will be a new Jerusalem and a new temple. Kingship will be renewed with the true and ultimate ideal Davidic prince. The creation paradigm is repeated in many and varied ways to portray the new creation to come.

Creation, then, has set the pattern of the kingdom of God. Ruling over this kingdom as the vicegerent of the sovereign creator is the son of God. After the fall, the grace of God anticipates a new creation that involves a redemptive event applied to sinners who have died with Adam. The message of this renewal is conveyed as a series of covenants.

The son of God, therefore, is first of all Adam, then the nation of Israel, and then this nation's royal representative who is the son of David. Each exodus event[3] is portrayed as a rebirth of the nation of God's people. As redemptive history progresses, the imagery of rebirth and resurrection becomes more vivid. However, the exodus from Egypt was immediately dogged by Israel's unbelief. Even after temporary exile in the wilderness, the possession of the Promised Land was clouded with those failures recounted in the book of Judges. But when the prophets promise an end to the Babylonian exile, the picture becomes clearer and less ambiguous. Indeed, the prophetic projection of the glory to be revealed on the great day of the Lord contains little ambiguity as to its perfection and permanence.

---

[3] The biblical emphasis is on the exoduses from Egypt and Babylon, but we also see overtones of exodus in Israel's move from the wilderness into the Promised Land.

The experience of the return from Babylonian exile, as recounted in Ezra and Nehemiah, comes nowhere close to matching the prophetic visions of renewal. The three prophets who wrote after the exile,[4] Haggai, Zechariah, and Malachi, made clear that the nation restored under the Persians did not meet the prophetic expectations. The Old Testament comes to an end without complete renewal having taken place. The ensuing centuries of Persian, Greek, and then Roman authority simply did not fulfill expectations—if anything, they made them more remote by increasing the sufferings of the Jews.

What, then, is the hope that the prophets have spoken of? God's salvation that his people will experience is declared to be perfect, glorious, and forever. The creation paradigm is recalled in various ways in prophetic eschatology. Isaiah speaks of a new Eden and a new heaven and earth (Isa. 51:3; 65:17). Ezekiel describes how the land will become a new Eden (Ezek. 36:35–38). He also links the temple with a new Eden and depicts a river of life emanating from a new temple yielding Eden-like fruitfulness (Ezek. 47:1–12). All of the elements that make up the pattern of redemption and renewal in Israel's history are given expression in various prophetic oracles. These include creation/land, covenant, people/nation, king, Jerusalem, and temple. Restoration from exile precedes these events. And the temple, let us remember, includes the instruments and agents of atonement and mediation between God and his people. Every one of these elements involves an anointed human who stands for the many, either as prophet, priest, or king—each linked with the son of God as vicegerent over the kingdom.

To this mediator, then, we now turn.

We have thus far noted the general themes of creation and renewal that are repeated in the Old Testament. Anthony Petterson

---

[4] Usually referred to as the "postexilic prophets."

has provided us with an insightful study of the growing resurrection vocabulary that flows from creation and restoration.[5] In other words, even when there is no clearly stated hope of general resurrection, there are many clues to the emergence of the expectation of life after death. Some may be content to suggest that certain New Testament applications of the Psalms to the resurrection of Jesus are made with the benefit of hindsight. Thus, it might be claimed that the resurrection of Jesus enables Peter and Paul to apply Psalm 16:10–11 as pointing to that resurrection (Acts 2:24–32; 13:35).

> For you will not abandon my soul to Sheol,
>   or let your holy one see corruption.
> You make known to me the path of life;
>   in your presence there is fullness of joy;
>   at your right hand are pleasures forevermore. (Ps. 16:10–11)

But we must understand that the psalmist was writing from a context filled with the unshakeable hope of God's promises being fulfilled forever. Even if he wrote of something less than rising from the grave, being restored to life in God's Promised Land is part of the developing resurrection theme.

One passage from the Old Testament Wisdom Literature should be noted. Despite the acknowledged difficulties in the Hebrew text, there is some agreement amongst the commentaries that Job 19:25–27 deals with Job's hope for vindication in the face of the accusations that his sufferings are deserved.

> For I know that my Redeemer lives,
>   and at the last he will stand upon the earth.

---

[5] Anthony Petterson, "Antecedents of the Christian Hope of Resurrection, Part 1: The Old Testament," *Reformed Theological Review* 59/1 (2000): 1–15.

And after my skin has been thus destroyed,
    yet in my flesh I shall see God,
whom I shall see for myself,
    and my eyes shall behold, and not another.

This passage may not yet represent a full comprehension of the resurrection of the body by Job. However, there are additional references to resurrection that occur in the Prophets.

Come, let us return to the LORD;
    for he has torn us, that he may heal us;
    he has struck us down, and he will bind us up.
After two days he will revive us;
    on the third day he will raise us up,
    that we may live before him. (Hos. 6:1–2)

Your dead shall live; their bodies shall rise.
    You who dwell in the dust, awake and sing for joy!
For your dew is a dew of light,
    and the earth will give birth to the dead. (Isa. 26:19)

But at that time your people shall be delivered, everyone whose name shall be found written in the book. And many of those who sleep in the dust of the earth shall awake, some to everlasting life, and some to shame and everlasting contempt. (Dan. 12:1–2)

In these passages the rising of the dead is understood as the recovery from the judgment of God to experience the promised blessings of redemption. This recovery may signify a national resurrection, but it is not divorced from the experience of the individual. It is much more than a national identity being reestablished.

Of all the resurrection passages in the Old Testament, none can surpass the graphic imagery of Ezekiel 37. It should be clear by now that distinctions between national resurrection or restoration and personal resurrection of dead persons who rise again to life are blurred once we acknowledge that what is being dealt with in the redemptive procedure is the problem of death that Adam brought upon his race. Robert Martin-Achard's classic study focuses on this progression of resurrection ideas that correlate with the comprehensive nature of the future hope.[6] Ezekiel 37 is part of this progressive revelation of this overall picture of redemption that will culminate in the resurrection of the Son of God that Paul speaks of in Romans 1:4.

The covenant that Ezekiel sees being fulfilled is the promise of the God who has declared that he restores life:

> See now that I, even I, am he,
>   and there is no god beside me;
> I kill and I make alive;
>   I wound and I heal;
>   and there is none that can deliver out of my hand.
>   (Deut. 32:39)

Ezekiel endorses this conviction that the curse upon Adam is in fact being addressed by salvation that will one day be fully revealed:

> Therefore prophesy, and say to them, Thus says the Lord GOD: Behold, I will open your graves and raise you from your graves, O my people. And I will bring you into the land of Israel. And you shall know that I am the LORD, when I open your graves, and raise you from your graves, O my people. And I will put my Spirit within you, and you shall live, and I will place you in your own land. Then you shall know that I am the LORD; I have spoken, and I will do it, declares the LORD. (Ezek. 37:12–14)

---

[6] Robert Martin-Achard, *From Death to Life: A Study of the Development of the Doctrine of the Resurrection in the Old Testament* (Edinburgh: Oliver and Boyd, 1960).

The fact that Ezekiel's words come in his oracle of the restoration of the exiles to their own land does not detract from the implications of the resurrection. The covenant with the son of God continues. On the one hand, the restoration will be a time when the people say: "This land that was desolate has become like the garden of Eden, and the waste and desolate and ruined cities are now fortified and inhabited" (Ezek. 36:35). On the other hand, the restoration is secured in that "my servant David shall be king over them, and they shall all have one shepherd" (Ezek. 37:24). God promises that he will raise his people from their graves and put his Spirit within them. It is impossible not to link this with Paul's reference to Jesus being declared the Son of God "in power according to the Spirit of holiness by his resurrection from the dead" (Rom. 1:4).

Resurrection, then, is an Old Testament sharpening of the focus that begins with creation. We see this right from the beginning in the fact that the death of Adam and Eve in their ejection from the garden is not the end. The covenants promise renewal for the people of God. The sons of Adam experience a series of deaths by exile from the Promised Land and, by the grace of God, a series of new creations or new births.

Of course, these only foreshadow the reality that is to come on the day of the Lord, when all believers are given invincible resurrection bodies. It is no accident that Christians came to think of the first day of the week, the day of resurrection, as the day of the Lord or the Lord's Day.[7] Israel, the son of God given new life at the exodus from Egypt, becomes the corporate reality represented by the son of God who is son of David. Restoration

---

[7]The phrase "the Lord's day" occurs only once in the New Testament, in Revelation 1:10. Sabbath keepers (Saturday worshipers) dispute the interpretation of this being the first day of the week. From early times, however, it was accepted in the church that the evidence for Sunday, the day of resurrection, is strong.

from the death of exile foreshadows the bodily resurrection of
the Son of God. His resurrection combines the national and the
personal elements foreshadowed in the Old Testament. In Acts
13:32–33 Paul declared that the promises of God are fulfilled in
the resurrection. These promises include the gracious work of the
Spirit to breathe new life into God's people. It is this resurrection
life that declares Jesus to be the Son of God.

One other point needs to be made. There are various terms
used in the New Testament to convey the idea of regeneration or new creation. Interestingly, the one Greek word that
literally means "regeneration" (*palingenesia*) occurs only in two
places. One of these is Titus 3:5 ("the washing of regeneration"), which does focus on personal regeneration through the
Holy Spirit.

The other, Matthew 19:28 ("the new world"), points us to the
ultimate regeneration of all things and the new kingdom of God:

> Jesus said to them, "Truly, I say to you, in the new world [*palin-
> genesia:* the regeneration], when the Son of Man will sit on his
> glorious throne, you who have followed me will also sit on twelve
> thrones, judging the twelve tribes of Israel."

This can only mean that the nation is restored and the faithful
remnant resurrected. The fact that Jesus couches this description
of the consummation of regeneration in Jewish apocalyptic terms[8]
does not obscure the fact that, as Son of Adam, he is describing the dominion of the resurrected people of God sharing the
rule with the Son of God. Many evangelical Christians seem to
think of regeneration purely in terms of their own new birth.

---

[8] Apocalyptic uses the kind of language, often highly symbolic, that we find in Daniel and the
book of Revelation. The word *apocalyptic* comes from a Greek word meaning "to reveal" and
refers to the revealing on earth of heavenly realities.

Yet regeneration is not only a profound personal experience; it is also as wide as the whole creation—the making of all things new (Rev. 21:5).

Sons of God (Galatians 4:4–7)

How does all this relate to *us* and our existence as sons of God?

When Jesus disputed with the Sadducees about the resurrection he linked resurrection to the status of sons of God:

> For they cannot die anymore, because they are equal to angels and are sons of God, being sons of the resurrection. But that the dead are raised, even Moses showed, in the passage about the bush, where he calls the Lord the God of Abraham and the God of Isaac and the God of Jacob. Now he is not God of the dead, but of the living, for all live to him. (Luke 20:36–38)

Those who are considered worthy of eternal life are sons of the resurrection and therefore sons of God. This connection is very similar to the one Paul highlights in Romans 1:3–4. We can join these realities thus: Jesus is declared to be Son of God through his resurrection; we are united to Jesus; our resurrection is established by the resurrection of Jesus. We are thus sons of God because we are sons of the resurrection.

This solidarity of believers with Christ as the Son of God is summed up in Paul's statement in Galatians 4:4–7:

> But when the fullness of time had come, God sent forth his Son, born of woman, born under the law, to redeem those who were under the law, so that we might receive adoption as sons. And because you are sons, God has sent the Spirit of his Son into our hearts, crying, "Abba! Father!" So you are no longer a slave, but a son, and if a son, then an heir through God.

The "fullness of time" here is clearly the time appointed for Jesus to come as God in the flesh. A similar phrase is used in Ephesians 1:10, and both passages recall the declaration of Jesus that "the time is fulfilled" in Mark 1:15. All three passages apply to the incarnation while also foreshadowing the consummation. Here in Galatians 4:4, his coming is described as God's sending forth his Son.

And lest there be any misunderstanding, he is born of a woman. His humanity is not an idealized reality that would render him unreachable, for he was born under the law so that we might receive sonship by adoption. We are not true sons by nature; we need to be adopted. But adoption is not a fictional relationship. God seals it by sending the Spirit of his true Son into our hearts so that we can respond as true sons with "Abba! Father!" We are true sons. (We might also note that sonship is not a gender issue. It concerns our status "in Christ"; our sonship is by adoption into his sonship. Gender-inclusive translations miss the point when they insist on "sons" being translated "children."[9])

This sonship should fill all believers, male or female, with confidence in their salvation. The passage referred to above is part of Paul's treatment of the Abrahamic covenant:

> Now the promises were made to Abraham and to his offspring. It does not say, "And to offsprings," referring to many, but referring to one, "And to your offspring," who is Christ. (Gal. 3:16)

The logic of Paul's argument, then, is that the relationship of Christ to Abraham has ramifications for us because of our relationship to Christ, as noted in the italicized section of the text below.

---

[9] Paul does use the phrase "children of God" (*tekna*) in Rom. 8:16, 21; Phil. 2:15.

Now before faith came, we were held captive under the law, imprisoned until the coming faith would be revealed. So then, the law was our guardian until Christ came, in order that we might be justified by faith. But now that faith has come, we are no longer under a guardian, *for in Christ Jesus you are all sons of God, through faith.* For as many of you as were baptized into Christ have put on Christ. There is neither Jew nor Greek, there is neither slave nor free, there is no male and female, for you are all one in Christ Jesus. And if you are Christ's, then you are Abraham's offspring, heirs according to promise. (Gal. 3:23–29)

The heart of Paul's argument here is that the promises concerning Abraham's offspring find their primary fulfillment in Christ. This is only one example of the role Jesus has in fulfilling the promises of God in the Old Testament (Acts 13:32–33; 2 Cor. 1:20; Eph. 1:10). The "meanwhile" period for God's people under the law is resolved when faith comes—that is, faith in Christ. Jesus *is* the offspring of promise; he *is* the Son of God. He is the one for the many so that all who believe in him are sons of God. This is another way of saying we are Abraham's offspring. So the argument goes: Jesus is Abraham's offspring; he is the son of God. Therefore all who are in Christ through faith are Abraham's offspring, the sons of God.

In Galatians 4, the argument continues: the Son of God comes into the world so that we can receive the same status (sons) as he has (Son). An aspect of this status is to be endowed with the Spirit of the Son so that, as he does, we address God as our Father. Similar to the adoption metaphor is the "authority" or "right" given to believers to become children of God (John 1:12).

Galatians 4:6 thus stands as central to our theology of prayer by describing prayer as the activity of God's sons. It speaks of the sovereignty of God in that he initiates the sending of his Son, and, as a result of this, we are adopted as sons. The logic of sharing this sonship status with Jesus is that God sends the Spirit of his Son into our hearts and we are consequently able to address God as our Father.

We also see the deeply Trinitarian nature of prayer in this text in Galatians. The basis of our prayer is the sonship of Jesus. The ground upon which prayer is offered with the confidence that the Father hears us is solely our union with Jesus. The source of our prayer is the Father's adoption of us as sons and the fact that he speaks to us first, just as he spoke first to Adam (Gen. 1:28–30). Prayer is initiated by God's word as he speaks to us; it is not generated by us. The enabling of prayer is from the Spirit of Jesus, who gives us the response of "Father."[10] Because Jesus is the Son of God, his Father always hears him, and it is this that gives us confidence that, in our union with Jesus, our prayer is heard. Paul makes a similar point in Romans 8:14–16:

> For all who are led by the Spirit of God are sons of God. For you did not receive the spirit of slavery to fall back into fear, but you have received the Spirit of adoption as sons, by whom we cry, "Abba! Father!" The Spirit himself bears witness with our spirit that we are children of God.

Paul here uses "child" (Gk. *teknon*) synonymously with "son" (Gk. *huios*). As stated in Galatians 4:6, we have the Spirit because we share the sonship of Jesus, and the Spirit enables us to address God as Father.

The principle of the one who stands for the many, which we have seen in the Old Testament from the outset, becomes important for our understanding of the union of the believer

---

[10] I have expounded this perspective in more detail in my book *Prayer and the Knowledge of God* (Leicester, UK: Inter-Varsity, 2003).

with Christ. The Pelagian[11] heresy, which says that we are all born innocent, really undermines the account in Genesis of the fall of mankind. If there is no corporate solidarity, so that "as in Adam all die," then everyone actually begins life as if innocent in Eden and must merely imitate Adam and learn to sin in order to be cast out (1 Cor. 15:22). The doctrine of original sin, on the other hand, expresses the scriptural fact that every member of the human race has been born outside the garden since Adam and Eve were thrown out of it.

The same principle operates in the corporate nature of the chosen people and is shown in the many ways that the one stands for the many. This principle does not cancel out individual responsibility. The whole nation came out of Egypt, but "with most of them God was not pleased, for they were overthrown in the wilderness" (1 Cor. 10:5). Israel's priest entered on behalf of all the people into the holy place and the presence of God. Because of the sacrifices he was the mediator of redemption. In the same way, the king represented the nation as the mediator of God's rule. The fortunes of the nation are seen by the writer of 1 and 2 Kings to depend on whether the king did that which was right or that which was evil in the eyes of the Lord. Evil kings prevailed, and the whole nation went into exile.[12]

When Jesus submitted to John's baptism of repentance, he did so as the representative of the true Israel. The word of approval after his baptism acknowledged him as the Son in whom God was well pleased. As we saw in chapter 2, "Son of God" was a way of describing Jesus as the true Adam and the faithful and obedient Israel. His resurrection demonstrated and pronounced his status as

---

[11] Pelagius was a British theologian who was vigorously opposed by Augustine in the early fifth century for his views that played down the seriousness of sin.
[12] Thus, even the reforms of a righteous king like Josiah could not avert the judgment on Judah because of the sins of Manasseh (2 Kings 23:26–27; Jer. 15:1–6).

Son of God, a fact completed in his ascension to the right hand of the Father. This exaltation is the return of the Son of God to Eden, which is defined by the presence of God. The people of God reach their goal and perfection in the ascension of Jesus.

We may well question such an assertion in that it seems to suggest that the church of God is reduced to one man, Jesus. However, this suggestion is not as strange as it may first appear. The New Testament goes on to indicate that just as in Adam all die, "so also in Christ shall all be made alive" (1 Cor. 15:22). One man sinned, and all who are "in him" die. One man suffered righteously, and all who are "in him" are made alive. The resurrection not only shows Jesus to be the Son of God but also focuses on the new creation. Union with Christ by faith, described by Paul as being "in Christ," unites us to the new creation:

> Therefore, if anyone is in Christ, [he is] a new creation. The old has passed away; behold, the new has come. All this is from God, who through Christ reconciled us to himself and gave us the ministry of reconciliation. (2 Cor. 5:17–18)

The bracketed verb *to be* ("he is") is not in the Greek and is supplied by translators to make a proper English sentence. But does the inserted pronoun *he* refer to "anyone" or to "Christ"? It may seem logical to say the former, but could not this phrase be translated "[there is] a new creation" in that the one who is in Christ is a new creation solely because Christ is the new creation, and shown to be so by his resurrection from the dead? This agrees with Peter's word that God "has caused us to be born again to a living hope through the resurrection of Jesus Christ from the dead" (1 Pet. 1:3). Peter sees our new birth as the result of the resurrection of Jesus. Regeneration, new birth, and new creation are all linked to the resurrection.

Everything Paul says about our justification by grace, through faith in Jesus Christ, hangs on this principle of our solidarity with Christ, our union with him by faith. This is crucial to Paul's theology, so much so that he goes beyond the language of our faith in Christ, our representative and substitute, to speak of the many (the believers) as if they were corporately with or in Christ in his saving life and death (Rom. 6:3–11; Eph. 2:5–6; Col. 3:1–4). The corporate reversal from Adam's death to Christ's life means that we of Adam's line died with Christ, and with him we were raised to life. Because he is our substitute, our actual personal experience is to watch from afar as he suffers and dies on our behalf to bear the judgment on our sin. Because he is our representative, what he achieves is imputed to us. This dying for sin is not our empirical experience but is a declaratory word from God that we receive by faith. In other words, God tells us that believers have died with Christ. Our union with Christ, along with the imputation to us of his life and death, enables Paul to use the language he does:

> But the free gift is not like the trespass. For if many died through one man's trespass, much more have the grace of God and the free gift by the grace of that one man Jesus Christ abounded for many. (Rom. 5:15)

> We were buried therefore with him by baptism into death, in order that, just as Christ was raised from the dead by the glory of the Father, we too might walk in newness of life. For if we have been united with him in a death like his, we shall certainly be united with him in a resurrection like his. (Rom. 6:4–5)

> I have been crucified with Christ. It is no longer I who live, but Christ who lives in me. And the life I now live in the flesh I live

> by faith in the Son of God, who loved me and gave himself for me. (Gal. 2:20)

> But God, being rich in mercy, because of the great love with which he loved us, even when we were dead in our trespasses, made us alive together with Christ—by grace you have been saved—and raised us up with him and seated us with him in the heavenly places in Christ Jesus. (Eph. 2:4–6)[13]

What Paul states about believers in these passages (and others) are the things that belong to the Son of God, who is our representative and substitute. Our status is imputed to us on the basis of the merits and achievements of Jesus—his life, his death, his resurrection, and his exaltation. Our union with him is such that our assurance of acceptance by God and, therefore, of salvation, is based upon his exaltation as the Son of God.

All that the Old Testament says about the death and restoration of the people of God finds its fulfillment in Jesus as the representative Son of God. Ezekiel spoke of the Holy Spirit as the power of the resurrection of the nation of Israel (Ezek. 37:11–14). Paul declares that the same Spirit is the power of the Son of God's resurrection (Rom. 1:4). Now we see that the resurrection and exaltation of Jesus are the grounds for the bestowal of the Spirit on his disciples at Pentecost and ever after (Acts 2:30–33). In order to be filled with the Spirit the disciples fulfilled no conditions or achieved no special level of holiness. They were just there as believers (Luke 24:49; Acts 1:4; 2:1). The baptism of the Spirit belongs to and is experienced by every believer, because Christ has fulfilled on our behalf all the conditions for the reception of this baptism.

---

[13] See also Rom. 4:1–5; 2 Cor. 5:21.

The unbreakable link between the sonship of Jesus and the Holy Spirit also pertains to our sonship in Christ. Our adoption is not merely a suppositional relationship. Imputation of Christ's righteousness is not pretense. Our union with Christ is real because of the ministry of his Holy Spirit:

> For all who are led by the Spirit of God are sons of God. For you did not receive the spirit of slavery to fall back into fear, but you have received the Spirit of adoption as sons, by whom we cry, "Abba! Father!" The Spirit himself bears witness with our spirit that we are children of God, and if children, then heirs—heirs of God and fellow heirs with Christ, provided we suffer with him in order that we may also be glorified with him. (Rom. 8:14–17)

Again, what belongs to Jesus as Son of God belongs to all who believe. We are fellow heirs with Christ. One difference would seem to present itself: our relationship to the Father is by grace and adoption as sons. The sonship we have is derived from Christ's sonship. Our acceptance with the Father is based on the Father's acceptance of Jesus. His acceptance is due to his merits as the faithful, obedient, and true Son of God. Thus, only if the Father should repudiate the sonship of Jesus could our sonship be repudiated. Only if the Father no longer hears the Son would he stop hearing the prayers of those who are "in Christ." Paul goes on in Romans 8 to talk about the final undoing of Adam's rebellion. The reversal of the curse that befell the whole creation will be achieved when we experience the final redemption of our bodies in the resurrection:

> For the creation was subjected to futility, not willingly, but because of him who subjected it, in hope that the creation itself will be set free from its bondage to corruption and obtain the

freedom of the glory of the children of God [Gk. *ton teknon tou theou*]. For we know that the whole creation has been groaning together in the pains of childbirth until now. And not only the creation, but we ourselves, who have the firstfruits of the Spirit, groan inwardly as we wait eagerly for adoption as sons [Gk. *huiothesian*], the redemption of our bodies. (Rom. 8:20–23)

Once again we encounter the creation–new creation dynamic that is integral to the destiny of the sons of God. This will be consummated by the resurrection of our bodies, their final redemption. The Spirit that raised Jesus is the Spirit who will raise us (Rom. 8:11) and who intercedes for us who believe (Rom. 8:26–27). This logically leads to one of the greatest passages of Christian assurance in the whole of Scripture:

And we know that for those who love God all things work together for good, for those who are called according to his purpose. For those whom he foreknew he also predestined to be conformed to the image of his Son, in order that he might be the firstborn among many brothers. And those whom he predestined he also called, and those whom he called he also justified, and those whom he justified he also glorified. What then shall we say to these things? If God is for us, who can be against us? (Rom. 8:28–31)

Little wonder that Paul exults in the truth that, we having God on our side, none can prevail against us. The eternal purpose of God was to predestine his elect to be conformed to the image of his Son. The process of calling, justification, and glorification is presented as, in one sense, already completed. God's predestination is sovereign and cannot be thwarted. That many are to be conformed to the image of the Son means that he is not alone in this sonship. He is the firstborn of the many who are his brothers.

Paul uses similar imagery in reference to the resurrection:

> But each in his own order: Christ the firstfruits, then at his coming those who belong to Christ. (1 Cor. 15:23; see also Col. 1:18)

The firstfruits of the crops that were offered to God by Israel did not consist in the fruit of a special early planting (Lev. 23:10). They were the first of the produce harvested from the general planting. When the firstfruits were harvested, the general harvest had begun. *Christ's resurrection, declaring him to be Son of God, was the beginning of the general resurrection* (1 Cor. 15:20–23). There are two distinct phases to the one harvest, at different points in history, but it is still a single harvest. When we celebrate the resurrection of Jesus and declare "Christ is risen!" we express our confidence in our own resurrection and revealing as sons of God (Rom. 8:19). The general resurrection has begun.

Living by Faith in the Son of God (Galatians 2:19–20)

Being a Christian means having faith in Jesus, the Son of God. But how much does one need to know about the real Jesus in order to have saving faith in him?

Some would emphasize it as *having faith* in Jesus, as if faith were an entity in itself and something that we produce from within ourselves. You will sometimes hear the statement, "You've got to have faith!" But, faith in what? The New Testament emphasizes the matter as having faith *in Jesus*. Faith is not something we produce in a vacuum; it is what happens when the Spirit enables us to see Jesus as worthy of our trust and confidence.

We can assume nothing about what the name Jesus Christ means to the unchurched. Added to this growing ignorance that characterizes an increasingly secular age is the apparent confusion among many Christians about the necessary content of the gospel message. Does it make any sense at all to call people to believe in Jesus, to make their decision for Jesus, or to receive him as their personal savior, when they have no idea why they need to do any of these things, or have not been told anything substantial about who Jesus is and what he has done? What did the Philippian jailer actually understand when Paul and Silas answered his cry for help with, "Believe in the Lord Jesus, and you will be saved"? We are told that "they spoke the word of the Lord to him and to all who were in his house" (Acts 16:31–32). Presumably they informed him about Jesus and his saving work before he believed.

It should be clear from this study that the names and titles of Jesus are far more significant in this matter than functioning as mere labels. Paul's letters leave little doubt as to what he understands the gospel to entail. It involves the sovereign, saving work of God for us in Christ. This work *for us* needs to be distinguished from the work of God *in us*, which includes the Holy Spirit enabling us to respond in faith (Acts 13:48; 16:14). It follows that we need to spell out the work of God for us in Christ if people are to respond appropriately to him as savior. So it is relevant to ask about the role of the names and titles of Jesus as grounds for faith in him.

Sometimes we find qualifying clauses to the name or title given to Jesus that clarify the content of the gospel, for example:

> I have been crucified with Christ. It is no longer I who live, but Christ who lives in me. And the life I now live in the flesh I live by faith in the Son of God, who loved me and gave himself for me. (Gal. 2:19–20)

Here the Son of God is described in terms of his love and self-giving. Paul also finds it quite natural to switch between the sovereign work of God and our responsibility in the life of faith. Living by faith in the Son of God involves two things. First, there is the fact that the Son of God "loved me and gave himself for me." Second, my faith is shaped and defined by this Son, who has done this for me. To have faith is to believe in this Son, not in some vague and undefined person. The sovereign work of God *for us* leaves us in one sense quite passive. We do not cooperate in this work; indeed we cannot, since the foundational work was done *for* us, *without* us, and *before* we were here to have any part in it. When Paul says, "I have been crucified with Christ," he uses a passive verb. He speaks of what was done for him as also done to him. Once again he speaks of a believer, in this case himself, as participating in the central event of the crucifixion of Jesus.

As far as we know, Paul was not present when Jesus died. Yet he speaks as if he had been there and shared passively in the event. He speaks of his readers in a similar way in Ephesians 2:5–10. And he does it again in Colossians 3:1–5, where he moves from the indicative (what is or what has been done) to the imperative (what we should do because of our involvement in what has been done). This grammatical distinction is vital to our proper understanding of the text. Note the following passage in which the indicatives (indicating what happened) govern the imperatives (what should be done as a result):

> If then you have been raised with Christ, seek the things that are above, where Christ is, seated at the right hand of God. Set your minds on things that are above, not on things that are on earth. For you have died, and your life is hidden with Christ in God. When Christ who is your life appears, then you also will appear with him in glory. Put to death therefore what is earthly in you. (Col. 3:1–5)

The "if" in "If you have been raised with Christ" does not express uncertainty about a believer's being raised with Christ. We could justifiably translate this Greek expression as, "It being the case that [or simply "since"] you have been raised with Christ, then you should seek the things that are above." So Paul's indicatives in this passage are: you have been raised with Christ; he is seated at the right hand of God; you have died and your life is hidden with Christ in God; Christ is your life; when he appears, you also will appear with him in glory. The imperatives that stem from these are: seek the things that are above; set your minds on the things that are above; and put to death what is earthly within you. In Galatians 2:19–20 the indicative links Paul, and thus the believer, to the death of Christ in the same way as in Colossians 3.

In short, the significance of Jesus's being called the "Son of God" is important for understanding what it means to live by faith in him. This Jesus is the Christ to whom Paul (and every true believer) is united in the crucifixion. Thus Paul can say that he has been crucified with Christ. This union is a union by faith, enabled and sealed by the Spirit. Paul's distinct way of speaking here and in passages such as Ephesians 2:1–8 is not the natural way that we would speak about ourselves. Yet it is important to grasp this way of speaking about our faith union with Christ. That we died with Christ is an important part of Paul's exposition of our saving relationship with him, as it has ramifications for our ongoing Christian lives and our eternal destiny:

> How can we who died to sin still live in it? Do you not know that all of us who have been baptized into Christ Jesus were baptized into his death? We were buried therefore with him by baptism into death, in order that, just as Christ was raised from the dead by the glory of the Father, we too might walk in newness of life. (Rom. 6:2–4)

So you also must consider yourselves dead to sin and alive to God in Christ Jesus. (Rom. 6:11)

The argument is simply this: if we have died with Christ, then we have died to sin, and so we cannot go on living in it as we once did.

Returning to Paul's argument in Galatians 2, we ask if his reference to living by faith in "the Son of God" involves a deliberate and significant choice of the name. I suggest that Paul does make a purposeful choice here. He says the law has put him to death in that no one can be justified by works of the law. This is not the law's failure but ours since we are incapable of keeping the law. Being crucified with Christ means Paul is free from the law so that he might live to God. How? His bodily existence continues but under a different principle. Now he lives by faith in the Son of God. He is counted as having died, in the person of his representative and substitute, and thus as having paid the penalty for his sin. He is free from the condemnation of the law.

Thus far our study of "son of God" has shown a predominant reference to the fact that God the Son has become the incarnate Son of God. Later we must examine the reverse emphasis, namely that the incarnate Son is in fact God the Son. At this point, we can highlight the role of the incarnate Son of God. He has come to do for the sons of fallen Adam what they cannot do for themselves so that they are made sons of God.

Paul's references to our union with Christ—in his life, suffering, death, resurrection, and ascension—focus on the God who, for our sake, became a man. I have already referred to the heresy called "Docetism," which could not accept the direct union of God and man. We see this error repudiated in 1 John 4:1–3, which refers to the claim that Jesus has not come in the flesh, that he is not truly human, as the spirit of the antichrist.

Centuries later, when the eighteenth-century Enlightenment began to affect the thinking of the Christian church and liberalism attempted to undermine the supernatural dimension of the biblical message, many started to doubt the full deity of Jesus. That Jesus was regarded as a man but not as God would seem to be the problem that faced us from the eighteenth century onward. In more recent times, some Christians have overreacted to this emphasis and have stressed the deity of Jesus to the neglect of his humanity. But Docetism (Jesus is God but not man) and Ebionism (Jesus is man but not God) both destroy the gospel of the God-man. Furthermore, those who deny the deity of Jesus can also easily deny his true humanity by doubting the historicity of his life and, thus, reduce him to an ethical ideal. On this view, it becomes unimportant whether Jesus lived or died according to the Gospel records. What matters is the ethical and existential message of the stories about him; how the story affects my understanding of myself.

A more subtle distortion of the gospel comes with the overplaying of the role of the Spirit in Christian living. When the Spirit is divorced from the Word and from the gospel event of Jesus, we can end up with a docetic Jesus. The belief in a docetic Jesus can then lead to us thinking about ourselves and the Bible in a docetic way. Our humanity and that of the Bible is thus largely ignored. Instead of living by faith in the Son of God, we bow to the mistaken view that we must progress beyond the gospel to live by the Spirit as if he acts independently of the gospel. The docetic Christian is one who has lost sight of the role of our human responsibility to think through issues and to make godly decisions.[14] Instead of valuing our humanity, the Holy Spirit's leading is appealed to in unbiblical ways that allow no discussion

---

[14] We see this in the evangelical slogan, popular in some circles: "I am just a suit of clothes that Jesus wears."

or possibility of error in our decision making, because it ends up as the Spirit's decisions and not ours.

A docetic approach to the Bible is one that allows any text to have any meaning to which we might consider ourselves led by the Spirit. The human dimension of the Bible is ignored so that the careful exegesis of passages and a sound hermeneutic are regarded as unspiritual impositions on the Word of God.[15] What the Spirit makes the text mean to me is what it means! It is true for me even if it isn't true for you. What is worse is that any fanciful interpretation of Scripture is then attributed to the Holy Spirit's leading. But the Word is inspired by the Spirit, and his leading is always testable against the responsible exegesis of the Word.

Paul would have none of this Docetism. His ongoing bodily existence is lived by faith in the Son of God. The sonship of Jesus in this sense goes back, as we have seen, to the creation and to Adam. It is firmly anchored in the redemptive history of Israel, the son of God, and in God's promises to the son of David, who is also the son of God. Paul does not regard his bodily life as a matter of enduring this unwanted material burden and encumbrance until such time as he can divest himself of it and enter the pure life of the spirit. He is fully aware that his gospel does not hold out the Gnostic hope of the immortality of the soul, as the ancient Greeks expected. Rather he looks forward to the resurrection from the dead of the whole person—body, mind, and soul.

Let us now consider further the significance of "son of God" from the angle of our lives as Christian believers. Jesus

---

[15] "Hermeneutics" is the term used to cover the interpretation of the text. We engage in interpretation every time we seek to understand any communication, verbal or written. I have dealt with the matter in my book *Gospel-Centered Hermeneutics: Biblical Theological Foundations and Principles* (Downers Grove, IL: Apollos, 2006).

the Son of God mediates our salvation and our permanent relationship with our God. "For there is one God, and there is one mediator between God and men, *the man* Christ Jesus" (1 Tim. 2:5). Paul justifiably could have said "the God-man Christ Jesus." But he referred to the mediator as human. We have seen that "Son of God" is the title above all that emphasizes the fact that the Mediator-Savior is human. Jesus did not come to save only our souls (in the narrow sense of that word, distinct from our minds and bodies) but to save us as whole people. What is more, as we have seen, the Son of God came to restore the whole of creation. The bookends of the biblical narrative are creation (Genesis 1–2) and new creation (Revelation 21–22). The consummation of human history involves the new heaven and the new earth. New Testament eschatology teaches Christians to look forward to bodily resurrection and to eternal bliss on the new earth.

Christians are therefore sadly robbed of their heritage when they are not taught the significance of the bodily resurrection and the bodily ascension of Jesus. It is a shame when we fail to comprehend the true destiny of believers by holding to some vague idea of eternal bodiless existence in heaven. We can appear to have nothing to say about the creation and our dominion over it or about care for our world and our bodies. Is it any wonder that many secular thinkers regard Christianity as vacuous and irrelevant, if not downright mischievous?

Living by faith in the Son of God means living our lives, by God's grace, consistently with the nature of Christ's achievements for his people. It means having full assurance about the comprehensive nature of what he has achieved as the fulfiller of all the promises of God and all the expectations that arise because of the revelation of God's purposes in the Old Testament. Without growth toward that goal we will be in danger of uncertainty about our own salvation. As Paul says, "Faith comes from hearing, and hearing through the word of Christ" (Rom. 10:17). Faith, and a consequent assurance, must be based on knowing who it is that we have faith in. This includes living in fellowship with him. This is a matter of trust, and trust can remain only when we know the trustworthiness of the one we trust. That is why knowing the significance of the various names and titles that are applied to Jesus is important in our pursuit of maturity in our faith.

"I Will Be His God and He Will Be My Son" (Revelation 21:7)

Although the title "son of God" is rare in Revelation, the titles and images that relate to the redemptive process summed up in that title are everywhere. One of the keys to understanding the book of Revelation is the vision of the one who is qualified to open the seals of the scrolls and to reveal the truths therein. He is the Lion of the tribe of Judah, the Root of David who has conquered (Rev. 5:5).

Yet when John looks to see this conqueror, it is not the Lion that he sees but "a Lamb standing, as though it had been slain" (Rev. 5:6). This latter imagery is on first sight curious: how does a slain lamb stand? Surely, only through resurrection. This directs our focus to one of the features of the book of Revelation: it constantly refers to the Christ in terms that are drawn from the Old Testament.[16]

At the heart of Revelation, then, is the Lion who has conquered, who is also the Lamb who was slain. This motif of his conquest as the Lion means that those who remain faithful to

---

[16] See my book *The Gospel in Revelation*, in *The Goldsworthy Trilogy* (Milton Keynes, UK: Paternoster, 2000).

him are also conquerors. God Almighty has taken his power and begun to reign (Rev. 11:17). The saints have conquered Satan by the blood of the Lamb (Rev. 12:11).

The consummation comes with the final vision of the new heaven and the new earth in Revelation 21–22. All the creation themes are recalled in this grand climax. God now dwells with his people in the Jerusalem from heaven; they are his people and he is their God. Thus the covenant is fulfilled (Rev. 21:3). Because God is in fact amongst them, as he was with Adam in the garden, there is no temple in the new city of Jerusalem (Rev. 21:22). The temple symbolically represented the presence of God with his people, who were outside the garden. There was always the element of separation between God and his people expressed in the symbolism of the tabernacle and the temple; but no longer.

Redemptive events, such as the exodus and the return from exile, signal regeneration and resurrection. Here in the consummation God declares that he makes all things new (Rev. 21:5). All the great themes that have been linked with Jesus as the Son of God reach their ultimate fulfillment in these final visions. Everything summed up in the biblical themes of the new creation and our regeneration is seen as reaching its eternal goal. The believer, the one who overcomes, achieves the definitive expression of sonship of God (Rev. 21:7). Throughout the book John refers to the risen Jesus as "the Lamb." His constant use of the images and symbols of the action of God in Old Testament salvation history remains to the end. It is fitting, then, that one of his last descriptions of the perfected believer is with the words of the Davidic covenant:

> The one who conquers will have this heritage, and I will be his God and he will be my son. (Rev. 21:7; see 2 Sam. 7:14)

It is also fitting that within the context of the new creation, Jesus's last words of self-description are, "I am the root and the descendant of David, the bright morning star" (Rev. 22:16). Paul tells us that we have been predestined to be conformed to the image of the Son of God (Rom. 8:29). Here in Revelation's final vision of glory, we see the fullness of this being conformed to the image of the Son of God. It is the conquest of sin, Satan, and death that brings the believer to this ultimate transformation. John will not let us resolve the ambiguity of our earthly existence by dissolving it into some shapeless and ghostly existence. The risen and ascended Christ will be the incarnate Son of God for eternity, and believers will be defined by his image for eternity. It will be our eternal blessedness that we are the inheritors of the kingdom of God by grace and adoption as sons.

God's eternal plan never included the human race locked in the garden of Eden with the potential for self-destruction. Rather, it always included the work of Christ and his gospel, with a redeemed people in the new creation. This is the Sabbath rest for the people of God (Heb. 4:9–10). Revelation reminds us that the eternal life that is God's gift to believers is structured. We cannot comprehend much of what the promises of God speak of. "Heaven," "glory," "to be with Christ," "eternal life," and any other terms we use to describe what is in store for the believer all stretch our imagination to the limit. No doubt there are many, many surprises ahead for us that we can only dimly imagine now. The symbolism of the book of Revelation only increases the mystery. Yet the information we have, clothed though it may be in all kinds of symbols and images, assures us of an essential continuity with, and renewal of, the life already begun with Christ, the Son of God.

Son of God and God the Son

One matter remains. In distinguishing between the Son of God of redemptive history and God the Son, the eternal second person of the Trinity, I have not wanted in any way to separate them. Distinction can easily lead to separation.

There is a kind of ambiguity expressed in a number of Old Testament texts relevant to our study. These foreshadow the fact that the Son of God revealed in the New Testament may have his human ancestors, but he is never merely human. We cannot ignore the fact that Jesus the Son of God is also eternally God the Son, the second person of the Trinity. This development appears in passages that are applied to Jesus in the New Testament. These passages closely link the human and the divine and even suggest that they are one and the same person. Psalm 2:7 indicates a unique relationship of the Son to the Lord God:

> I will tell of the decree:
> The LORD said to me, "You are my Son;
>   today I have begotten you."

In Psalm 110:1 both persons are called "Lord":

> The LORD says to my Lord:
>   "Sit at my right hand,
> until I make your enemies your footstool."

In Isaiah 9:6 the child is identified as God:

> For to us a child is born,
>   to us a son is given;
> and the government shall be upon his shoulder,
>   and his name shall be called

Wonderful Counselor, Mighty God,
    Everlasting Father, Prince of Peace. (Isa. 9:6)

In Ezekiel 34:15 God describes himself as the shepherd of Israel but goes on in verses 22–23 to nominate David as the shepherd of Israel:

> I myself will be the shepherd of my sheep, and I myself will make them lie down, declares the Lord GOD. . . . I will rescue my flock; they shall no longer be a prey. And I will judge between sheep and sheep. And I will set up over them one shepherd, my servant David, and he shall feed them: he shall feed them and be their shepherd.

Jesus, who is both God and the Son of David, fulfills this role as the Good Shepherd (John 10:1–30).

The question remaining to be addressed is whether there are instances of the "son of God" that point us to the eternal deity of the Christ. In chapter 2 of this study, we examined John's use of the title as pointing to the deity of Jesus more overtly than the way in which the three Synoptic Gospels present it. If my conclusions are correct, the title "son of God" is mostly tied to the incarnate God, Jesus, and his historical predecessors in the Old Testament. But this in no way precludes the divine emphasis in other places. And it in no way precludes the clear evidence that *this Son of God is indeed God the Son from all eternity*. We would expect that a true mediator should share the essence of both parties to be reconciled. And so it turns out. The real saving role of the mediator between God and men is exercised by the one who is true God and true man.

The preexistence of Christ as God the Son is not really the subject of this study. But we are concerned to know if "son of

God" is a title used to point specifically to the deity of Jesus. Is "son of God" the same as "the Son," and is it implied by references to "the Father"? If so, it would seem to be relevant to the question of deity. Considering God's Son to begin with, Paul is very clear about the Son as central to the whole notion of Israel's redemptive history. But his terminology sometimes makes us look again at the Son. So in Galatians 4:4 the Son is born of a woman, but, on the other hand, he is "sent" by God (Rom. 8:3; Gal. 4:4) and "revealed" (Gal. 1:16). As W. G. Kümmel suggests, passages like this show that Jesus was God's Son before he was born of a woman.[17]

It is conceivable that John's Gospel, which contains many passages that assert or imply the deity of Jesus, also contains "son of God" occurrences that remain distinct in their emphasis on the incarnate Jesus in history. In chapter 2 of this study, I argued that "son of God" in John tends to occur in harmony with other kinds of sonship titles that belong to John's overall perspective of the God-man. It is not a case of one or the other but simply where the focus lies in any given occurrence.

Another distinction needs to be made in this matter. The title "Son of God" may have been used by some of the contemporaries of Jesus without any sense that it implied that he was God. At the same time, the Gospel writers put the reporting of such instances into a context that takes us beyond the conviction that Jesus is merely the human messiah figure of the Old Testament. It is difficult to avoid the conclusion that all four Gospels present Jesus in such a way that the contemporaries of Jesus, who spoke of him as Son of God, spoke better than they knew.[18] John has theologized on the title more than the others. None of the references to "son

---

[17] W. G. Kümmel, *Theology of the New Testament* (London: SCM, 1974), 160.
[18] This is argued by Thomas R. Schreiner, *New Testament Theology* (Grand Rapids, MI: Baker Academic, 2008), 241.

of God" in John's Gospel are without ambiguity meant to assert the deity of Jesus. But the picture is rather different when we link these with John's use of "son" in relationship with "Father." Thus, when Jesus healed the sick man on the Sabbath by the pool of Bethesda, the Jews disputed with him and wanted to kill him for calling God his Father (John 5:18),

> so Jesus said to them, "Truly, truly, I say to you, the Son can do nothing of his own accord, but only what he sees the Father doing. For whatever the Father does, that the Son does likewise. For the Father loves the Son and shows him all that he himself is doing. And greater works than these will he show him, so that you may marvel. For as the Father raises the dead and gives them life, so also the Son gives life to whom he will. The Father judges no one, but has given all judgment to the Son, that all may honor the Son, just as they honor the Father. Whoever does not honor the Son does not honor the Father who sent him. Truly, truly, I say to you, whoever hears my word and believes him who sent me has eternal life. He does not come into judgment, but has passed from death to life." (John 5:19–24)

It is difficult to miss the implication that Jesus is claiming equality with the Father.[19] John sustains this perspective throughout his Gospel. The Son is portrayed as the life giver; the one who will raise believers to life on the last day (e.g., John 6:35–40, 44, 54). He keeps his own people safe and gives them eternal life (e.g., John 5:39–40; 6:47, 51, 54, 58; 8:12; 10:7–10, 26–30). The unity of Father and Son is another theme in John:

> I give them eternal life, and they will never perish, and no one will snatch them out of my hand. My Father, who has

---

[19] D. A. Carson, *Jesus the Son of God* (Wheaton, IL: Crossway, 2012), 40–42.

given them to me, is greater than all, and no one is able to snatch them out of the Father's hand. *I and the Father are one.* (John 10:28–30)

Philip said to him, "Lord, show us the Father, and it is enough for us." Jesus said to him, "Have I been with you so long, and you still do not know me, Philip? *Whoever has seen me has seen the Father.*" (John 14:8–9)

So Jesus said to them, "Truly, truly, I say to you, the Son can do nothing of his own accord, but only what he sees the Father doing. For *whatever the Father does, that the Son does likewise.*" (John 5:19)

It is thus reasonable to propose that John moves us more directly to the position that the Son of God is himself God the Son. He is much more than the human messiah figure that the Jews expected.

We conclude that the Old Testament background to Jesus being called the Son of God begins to combine the attributes of the son of David with those of God himself. Thus, in Isaiah 9, the child born for the throne of David is called "Mighty God." In Ezekiel 34 both God and David are described as the "good shepherd" of Israel that is to come. In the New Testament, the title "Son of God" in the Synoptic Gospels is capable of being interpreted in terms of Jewish expectations of the coming Messiah, a descendant of David. But taken as whole books, the Gospels clearly aim much higher than the Jewish expectations. John's whole Gospel is framed by the divine Son. The Son is, on the one hand, the creating Word who is made flesh and, on the other hand, he is the Son who comes from the Father and is one with him.

The uniting of all things in Christ that Paul refers to in Ephesians 1:10 is another way of speaking of the effects of Christ's reconciling death on the cross. But, as I have already explained, the mediating role of the Son of God in salvation also points to his mediating role as God the Son. We noted that John begins his Gospel by referring to Jesus as the Word of God in creation (John 1:1–3). Hebrews identifies Jesus the prophet as also the creator and sustainer of all things (Heb. 1:1–2, 10). Oscar Cullmann proposes the incarnation as the center point of time because, since Christ's coming, Christians have understood time and history as reaching back from him to the beginning, with the creation, and as looking forward from him to the consummation with the new creation.[20] The Christ who came to earth two thousand years ago was the active Son in creation and redemption. He is mediator also of the new creation.

In this study I began by looking at the historical impact on the first Christians of Jesus's being called "son of God." It is clear that the coming of Jesus into this world changed the way God's people viewed the Old Testament. Not only did the apostles and the other New Testament authors reinterpret the Old Testament as being about Jesus, but they all followed the lead *given by Jesus himself* concerning his presence in the ancient events. Thus, the incarnation of Jesus as Son of God encourages us to see Jesus also as God the Son. Jesus is the figure who, above all, mediated creation and sustains it even now. Sentimentality often reduces Jesus to a tiny infant in a manger in Bethlehem. But he is nothing less than the creator and sustainer of the universe. When Paul reflects on Christ, he does not separate him from the central fact of redemptive history—the atoning death of Jesus that reconciles all things to himself:

---

[20] Oscar Cullmann, *Christ and Time: The Primitive Christian Conception of Time and History* (London: SCM, 1951).

He is the image of the invisible God, the firstborn of all creation. For by him all things were created, in heaven and on earth, visible and invisible, whether thrones or dominions or rulers or authorities—all things were created through him and for him. And he is before all things, and in him all things hold together. And he is the head of the body, the church. He is the beginning, the firstborn from the dead, that in everything he might be preeminent. For in him all the fullness of God was pleased to dwell, *and through him to reconcile to himself all things, whether on earth or in heaven, making peace by the blood of his cross.* (Col. 1:15–20)

We should note that this passage continues Paul's reflections on the great salvation experienced by his readers, and it expresses his prayer for them. He refers to their being transferred by God "to the kingdom of his beloved Son" (Col. 1:13–14). The passage that follows in Colossians 1:15–20 reflects on the attributes of this Son.

One final point in this passage is noteworthy.[21] Twice Paul refers to Jesus as "firstborn"; the first reference is to Jesus as "the firstborn of all creation" (Col. 1:15). This apparently qualifies the previous statement that the Son is the image of God. But this latter phrase presents certain difficulties if used to suggest that Jesus is no more than a created being and thus not God. Of course, his human nature is of the created order, for he would otherwise not be truly human. But let us consider the possible background to such a statement: Adam, though not designated "firstborn," was the first son of God in the original creation. Then Israel is designated "my firstborn son" in Exodus 4:22.

I have suggested that Israel, though not the original son of God, is God's firstborn in the new creation of a covenant peo-

---

[21] See Peter T. O'Brien, *Colossians, Philemon*, vol. 44, Word Biblical Commentary (Milton Keynes, UK: Word, 1987), 42–57.

ple, redeemed in the exodus, and dwelling in the new Eden, the Promised Land. Then Psalm 89:27 says of David, "I will make him the firstborn, the highest of the kings of the earth." This prophetic passage projects a view of the restored kingdom under the Davidic prince. The people of God are seen as represented by a new "firstborn" as they enter the new creation of the expected postexilic restoration. But the historical restoration from Babylon does not fulfill the prophetic expectation. Finally and ultimately, Jesus, who is the head of the new race of God's people, is the firstborn for the new creation. Paul refers to Jesus as "firstborn of all creation" and explains this in terms of the Son as creator and sustainer of all things. I suggest that Paul sees the Son, who is the God-man, as the firstborn of whom the others, Adam, Israel, and David, are but the shadows while the solid reality is Christ.

Paul's typology is similarly expressed in Colossians 2:16–17. Paul's reference to Jesus the Son as "firstborn of all creation" is but a variation of the assertions that "all things were created through him and for him" (Col. 1:16). It is also another way of saying that "he is the head of the body, the church" (Col. 1:18). The cosmic Christ is God the Son who fulfills the role of Son of God. All this means that *the actions of God in Jesus Christ fulfill all God's purposes for Adam's race.* God could have justly consigned the creation to nothingness, but his eternal purpose of grace was to bring to glory a race redeemed by Christ with him as the head, as the new Adam, as the true Israel, as the Son of David, and as the Son of God.

Summary and Conclusion

The doctrines of the Trinity and the incarnation of God can present ordinary Christians with problems at the level of personal faith and of corporate worship. It is difficult to try to define how we can speak about one God being three persons, and about one person called Jesus being both true God and true man. But these great truths will have bearing on our personal faith. They are not purely academic matters.

I have already identified some of the ancient heresies that have dogged the Christian faith throughout history. Each one has represented a failed attempt to resolve the mystery of one person with two distinct and complete natures. One approach attempted to solve the problem by a logic that reduced the person of Christ to a monistic being:[22] he was either divine spirit or mortal man, but he could not have been both. The other solution proposed a hybrid: he is either two persons, or he is neither fully one nor the other. So serious were these heresies that John labeled one such solution as the spirit of antichrist (1 John 4:1–3). Contrary to these false solutions, and put in simple terms: faith in Jesus should be faith in the Jesus presented in the Bible, the whole Bible, both Old and New Testaments. We are not justified by the purity of our doctrine, but our spiritual welfare can be compromised if we do not grow in the grace *and knowledge* of our Lord Jesus Christ (2 Pet. 3:18). Striving for doctrinal maturity is essential for a robust faith.

What we are faced with is a serious spiritual and pastoral problem. If one way of solving the mystery is to fall into serious error, we should be very concerned. The Bible points us in the direction of looking for the best way to preserve the mysteries of the Trinity and of the person of Jesus. How can ordinary Christians who are not trained in theological technicalities learn to understand what the Bible teaches us about God and Jesus? How can we speak about these realities without falling into error? One approach resolves the problem of God by saying Father, Son,

---

[22] Monism implies a single nature.

and Holy Spirit are not distinct persons but are simply different names we give to different activities of the one God. But the Bible teaches us that the three persons are indeed distinct, though not separated.

If God never did anything, he would still be eternally Father, Son, and Holy Spirit, three distinct persons in one God. Have you ever heard someone praying in a group who is not sure whom he should pray to? You may get the prayer addressed to "Father God," then to "Lord Jesus," and, finally, just to be evenhanded, to "O Holy Spirit." Well, why not? They are all God, and the one God at that. Praying to one person surely means praying to them all. Yet the New Testament pattern is that we pray to the Father through the mediation of the Son by the enabling power of the Holy Spirit. In other words, they are all God, but the distinct persons are not fused, and their roles are not interchangeable.

I have mentioned the Trinity for our consideration as we conclude this study, because it is closely linked with the person of Christ. The mystery in both is of the same order: one God who is three persons, and one person who has two natures. I will not repeat here my comments concerning the ancient heresies except to point out that in various ways, they are alive and well today. They can be implicit in the way we talk and think about our relationship with Christ even when we consciously subscribe to orthodox views. We may even dismiss any attempts to correct our unreflective and conversational attitude to Christ as hair-splitting and tedious. Feelings of piety over certain popular choruses that sound so spiritual may overshadow any suggestion that the sentiments expressed are misleading or even downright heretical.

Some defective concepts of Jesus Christ can be mentioned. The liberal Christianity that was given enormous impetus by Friedrich Schleiermacher in the early nineteenth century is alive and well today. It reduces Jesus to the most god-conscious of all human beings. The consequent ideas that Jesus was a wonderful human being, a good teacher, and a supreme human example of sacrificial love are all deficient and in effect redefine the human condition that can benefit by the ministry of such a diminished savior.

Unfortunately, evangelical reactions to such liberalism have sometimes included tendencies to the opposite heresies; in some circles, Jesus is conceived of as really not human at all. I hasten to add that mostly we evangelicals would deny that we hold to heretical views, even though we then express them in word and song! Thus the chorus ending, "You ask me how I know he lives; he lives within my heart." Yet to ignore the fact that Jesus is bodily in heaven and sends his Spirit to us (Rom. 8:9–11), is to be in danger of focusing our faith on what is happening within us rather than on the objective, finished work of the Son of God (Col. 3:1; Heb. 9:24). Soon our feelings and spiritual euphoria become the means for gauging our spiritual health and for having assurance of salvation. Faith then becomes faith in our feelings of having Jesus "in our hearts." We must remember that we know that Christ lives because the Bible tells us so, not because of a subjective feeling of having Jesus "in me." The same biblical word informs and assures us of the power of Christ in his gospel to save and to give us the grace of perseverance until our earthly life's end.

In chapter 2 I looked at some points of contact with "son of God" in the New Testament and observed the close interface between these and related titles of Jesus and their important Old Testament contexts. In chapter 3 I followed these New Testament prompts back into the Old Testament in order to examine their development within redemptive history. These links to Adam, Abraham, Israel, and Solomon as God's sons involved us with some other themes that are central to the biblical message. Jesus is thus understood to be fulfilling roles and summing up themes that tie him to the outworking of all of God's plans in creation and the history of redemption. With a more robust understanding of the title "son of God" in this broader context, I used chapter 4 to explore the significance of the sonship of Jesus and how it impacts the nature of our adoption as sons of God through faith in him.

Here is the bottom line to this study: *Jesus as Son of God is also God the Son, the eternal second person of the Godhead. But our salvation and eternal destiny depend on his being the incarnate one who is revealed as Son of God. Jesus, in his person and work, sums up the pattern of creation that establishes the nature of the kingdom of God.*

As Son of God, he is the new Adam, the new Israel, the new humanity. All the promises of God made to his people are fulfilled in Jesus: he is the new creation, the new Promised Land, the new Jerusalem, the new temple, and the new people of God. Thus, his resurrection signals the fact that he is the Son of God (Rom. 1:3–4) by demonstrating that he fulfills the promises of the Old Testament (Acts 13:32–33). Jesus as the Son of God defines our salvation as part and parcel of the renewal of all things: the new heaven and earth. Jesus as the Son of God, declared to be so by his resurrection, shows that our salvation is not merely the saving of our souls but the redemption of our whole being—body, mind, and soul—through our own resurrection. Jesus as the Son of God, by his death and resurrection, *was putting the whole universe back together from the futility to which it has been subjected* because of human rebellion against the Creator (Rom. 8:19–23). The consummation of this total regeneration is described in the book of Revelation as resurrection and the new heaven and earth. The dwelling place of God with his people is envisaged as a new Jerusalem let down from heaven to the new earth. The coming again of Jesus, our resurrection, and the renewal of all things is our certain expectation based on the fact that Jesus is the Son of God.

> Then I saw a new heaven and a new earth, for the first heaven and the first earth had passed away, and the sea was no more. (Rev. 21:1)

> And he who was seated on the throne said, "Behold, I am making all things new." (Rev. 21:5)

> He who testifies to these things says, "Surely I am coming soon." Amen. Come, Lord Jesus! (Rev. 22:20)

FOR FURTHER READING

Alexander, T. D. *From Eden to the New Jerusalem*. Nottingham, UK: Inter-Varsity, 2008.

Alexander, T. D., and Brian Rosner, eds. *New Dictionary of Biblical Theology*. Downers Grove, IL: InterVarsity, 2000.

Beale, G. K. *A New Testament Biblical Theology*. Grand Rapids, MI: Baker Academic, 2011.

Carson, D. A. *Jesus the Son of God*. Wheaton, IL: Crossway, 2012.

Clowney, E. P. *Preaching and Biblical Theology*. Grand Rapids, MI: Eerdmans, 1961.

———. *The Unfolding Mystery: Discovering Christ in the Old Testament*. Leicester, UK: Inter-Varsity, 1988.

Dempster, S. G. *Dominion and Dynasty: A Biblical Theology of the Hebrew Bible*. Downers Grove, IL: InterVarsity, 2003.

Dumbrell, W. J. *The End of the Beginning: Revelation 21–22 and the Old Testament*. Grand Rapids, MI: Baker, 1985.

———. *The Faith of Israel*. Grand Rapids, MI: Baker, 1988.

Gibson, R. J., ed. *Interpreting God's Plan*. Carlisle, UK: Paternoster, 1997.

Goldsworthy, G. *According to Plan*. Downers Grove, IL: InterVarsity, 2002.

———. *Christ-Centered Biblical Theology*. Downers Grove, IL: Inter-Varsity, 2012.

————. *Gospel and Kingdom.* In *The Goldsworthy Trilogy.* Milton Keynes, UK: Paternoster, 2000.

Hamilton, J. M. *God's Glory in Salvation through Judgment.* Wheaton, IL: Crossway, 2010.

Lawrence, M. *Biblical Theology in the Life of the Church.* Wheaton, IL: Crossway, 2010.

Longman, T. *Immanuel in Our Place.* Phillipsburg, NJ: P&R, 2001.

Peterson, D. *Christ and His People in the Book of Isaiah.* Leicester, UK: Inter-Varsity, 2003.

Roberts, V. *God's Big Picture: Tracing the Storyline of the Bible.* Leicester, UK: Inter-Varsity, 2003.

Wright, C. J. H. *Knowing Jesus through the Old Testament.* Downers Grove, IL: InterVarsity, 1992.

GENERAL INDEX

SCRIPTURE INDEX